Perfect Questions Perfect Answers

Books by
His Divine Grace A. C. Bhaktivedanta Swami Prabhupāda

Bhagavad-gītā As It Is
Śrīmad-Bhāgavatam
Śrī Caitanya-caritāmṛta
Kṛṣṇa, the Supreme Personality of Godhead
Teachings of Lord Caitanya
The Nectar of Devotion
The Nectar of Instruction
Śrī Īśopaniṣad
Light of the Bhāgavata
Easy Journey to Other Planets
Teachings of Lord Kapila, the Son of Devahūti
Teachings of Queen Kuntī
Message of Godhead
The Science of Self-Realization
The Perfection of Yoga
Beyond Birth and Death
On the Way to Kṛṣṇa
Rāja-vidyā: The King of Knowledge
Elevation to Kṛṣṇa Consciousness
Kṛṣṇa Consciousness: The Matchless Gift
Kṛṣṇa Consciousness: The Topmost Yoga System
Perfect Questions, Perfect Answers
Life Comes from Life
The Nārada-bhakti-sūtra (with disciples)
The Mukunda-mālā-stotra (with disciples)
Geetār-gān (Bengali)
Vairāgya-vidyā (Bengali)
Buddhi-yoga (Bengali)
Bhakti-ratna-boli (Bengali)
Back to Godhead magazine (founder)

Perfect Questions Perfect Answers

Conversations between
His Divine Grace
A. C. Bhaktivedanta Swami Prabhupāda
and Bob Cohen,
a Peace Corps worker in India

THE BHAKTIVEDANTA BOOK TRUST

Readers interested in the subject matter of this book are invited by the International Society for Krishna Consciousness to visit any ISKCON centre (see address list in back of book) or to correspond with the Secretary.

ISKCON Reader Services
P.O. Box 730
Watford, WD25 8ZE, United Kingdom
Tel: +44 (0) 1923 857244
Website: www.iskcon.org.uk

Perfect Questions, Perfect Answers was edited in 1973 by Śrīla Prabhupāda's disciple Jayādvaita Swami.

www.krishna.com

ISBN 1-84599-041-2

Printed in 2005

CONTENTS

His Divine Grace
A. C. Bhaktivedanta Swami Prabhupāda
Founder-*Ācārya* of the International Society for Krishna Consciousness

Introduction

A Perfectly Presumptuous Title?

Thirty-three years have passed since I sat near the Ganges River having the conversation described in this book. Since it was first published in 1976, I've shared many copies. Often it has been difficult to explain away a title that talks about my "perfect questions," for in 1972 I was twenty-two years old and quite far from perfection! Yet my partner in conversation, Śrīla Prabhupāda, suggested the title "Perfect Questions, Perfect Answers." And he was quite humble about himself. How did all this perfection come about?

My conservative Jewish family instilled in me an inner longing to understand God. Self-discovery and anti-war protests highlighted my college years, though in 1971 I did manage to graduate from Rensselaer Polytechnic Institute with a degree in chemistry. In that milieu of introspection and protest I became fascinated by the Hare Kṛṣṇa chant, which I first heard in the late '60s in Greenwich Village, and by the *Bhagavad-gītā,* the primer on *yoga.*

I learned that *yoga* means "union with God." The concepts of yoga attracted me, yet did not contradict the tenets of my upbringing. Still, the presentation of *yoga* in America troubled me. Every week the *New York Daily News* ran a centerfold of the latest Indian *guru* proclaiming his enlightenment to the world. Who could I trust? It seemed I needed to go to the source—mystical, faraway India. After college, the Peace Corps looked like an attractive way for me to explore India, live in a village, learn the language, and genuinely check out the *Gītā* and the chanting.

India was not as I had imagined. Abject poverty was, I discovered, for the most part an urban phenomenon. Though beggars swarmed through the cities, the countryside was lush with farms and peaceful villages of content people. A subtle, elusive transcendence permeated everything.

After starting my assignment as a high school science teacher in Bihar, I began visiting temples, mosques, and churches. It was disenchanting. The congregations were not seeking realization; they were seeking money, good luck, and prestige. It was the religious version of the '70s TV show "Let's Make a Deal." Had I traveled halfway around the world and endured "Delhi belly" only to find the same shallow values I had seen in materialistic America? I met various *gurus,* but remained unimpressed.

My existential search began to go up in smoke. In February 1972, I visited Calcutta during a school break. There were the Hare Kṛṣṇa devotees, mostly Westerners, chanting just as I'd seen them in Greenwich Village. They invited me to visit a retreat a hundred miles north of Calcutta. Deciding it fit in well with my quest, I agreed.

We took a train through the verdant Bengali countryside to Māyāpur, a beautiful spot near the Ganges River. Upon arriving, I discovered that Māyāpur was more of a planned retreat—for now it was a recently purchased rice paddy with tents and a hut. However, the paddy was near a sacred birthplace of the famed medieval saint Śrī Caitanya. And in the hut was the founder of the international Kṛṣṇa movement himself, an elderly gentleman named Śrīla Prabhupāda. His followers were busy running a soup kitchen for the many refugees from the recent Indo-Pakistani war. I plunked down in the men's tent and volunteered for the food relief effort.

There were sixty or so Kṛṣṇa followers, mostly American or European and under twenty-five years old. They were enthusiastic to say the least. Many were anxious to share their persuasion with the only English-speaking guest—me. However, I was invited to meet Śrīla Prabhupāda, and I sensed that this was the reason I had come to India.

Now for the "perfect questions" part that has caused me so much discomfort. The *Bhagavad-gītā* (the primer on transcendence) includes this admonition for a seeker:

Bob Cohen

"Just try to learn the truth by approaching a spiritual master. Inquire from him submissively and render service unto him. The self-realized souls can impart knowledge unto you because they have seen the truth." (4.34)

According to this instruction there are three qualifications for the novice:

1. visit the *guru*
2. inquire without challenging
3. assist the *guru* in some way

The *Gītā* suggests that the *guru* can "impart knowledge" when these three conditions are met.

My intention in visiting Śrīla Prabhupāda was to explore rather than contend. After meeting and studying many self-proclaimed instructors, I was extremely skeptical, yet Śrīla Prabhupāda's followers intrigued me.

Once I got past their zealousness, I found a genuine blend of mysticism and renunciation along with convincing explications. I resolved to spend my time with Śrīla Prabhupāda learning rather than challenging. Later on I could always decide to accept or reject what I had heard.

In this way I met the first and second of the *Gītā's* three credentials. The famine relief program of the Kṛṣṇa movement also occupied my day, so I was able to meet number three as well.

From Śrīla Prabhupāda's point of view I was following the *Gītā's* edicts: hence *Perfect Questions*. Meanwhile, Śrīla Prabhupāda answered my questions based on this prescription from the *Gītā* (4.2): "This supreme science was thus received through the chain of disciplic succession, and the saintly kings understood it in that way."

Śrīla Prabhupāda answered my questions based on the ancient system of disciplic succession—repeating what he had heard from previous authorities, and not making anything up. Thus I had *Perfect Answers* for my respectful questions, presented by a humble messenger of his predecessors.

The first conversation I had with Śrīla Prabhupāda was not recorded by his secretary. Therefore the book begins without our introductions and initial dialogue. All of the substantive matters begin with the second dialogue—the first chapter.

May reading my conversations with Śrīla Prabhupāda lead you to your own perfection.

—Bob Cohen

ONE

Kṛṣṇa, the All-Attractive

Māyāpur, India—February 27, 1972

Bob: What is the meaning of the name Kṛṣṇa?

Śrīla Prabhupāda: Kṛṣṇa means 'all-attractive.'

Bob: All-attractive.

Śrīla Prabhupāda: Yes. So unless God is all-attractive, how can He be God? A man is important when he is attractive. Is it not?

Bob: It is so.

Śrīla Prabhupāda: So, God must be attractive, and attractive for all. Therefore, if God has any name, or if you want to give any name to God, only 'Kṛṣṇa' can be given.

Bob: But why only the name Kṛṣṇa?

Śrīla Prabhupāda: Because He's all-attractive. Kṛṣṇa means 'all-attractive.' God has no name, but by His qualities we give Him names. If a man is very beautiful, we call him 'beautiful.' If a man is very intelligent, we call him 'wise.' So the name is given according to the quality. Because God is all-attractive, the name Kṛṣṇa can be applied only to Him. Kṛṣṇa means 'all-attractive.' It includes everything.

Bob: But what about a name meaning 'all-powerful'?

Śrīla Prabhupāda: Yes… Unless you are all-powerful, how can you be all-attractive?
Śyāmasundara [*Śrīla Prabhupāda's secretary*]: The name Kṛṣṇa includes everything.
Śrīla Prabhupāda: Everything. He must be very beautiful, He must be very wise, He must be very powerful, He must be very famous…
Bob: Is Kṛṣṇa attractive to rascals?
Śrīla Prabhupāda: Oh, yes! He was the greatest rascal also.
Bob: How is that?
Śrīla Prabhupāda: [*laughing*] Because He was always teasing the *gopīs*.
Śyāmasundara: Teasing?
Śrīla Prabhupāda: Yes. Sometimes when Rādhārāṇī would go out, Kṛṣṇa would attack Her, and when She would fall down—'Kṛṣṇa, don't torture Me in that way'—They would fall down, and Kṛṣṇa would take the opportunity and kiss Her. [*He laughs.*] So, Rādhārāṇī was very pleased, but superficially Kṛṣṇa was the greatest rascal. So unless rascaldom is in Kṛṣṇa, how could rascaldom exist in the world? Our formula of God is that He is the source of everything. Unless rascaldom is in Kṛṣṇa, it could not be manifest here, because He is the source of everything. But His rascaldom is so nice that everyone worships His rascaldom.
Bob: What about the rascals who are not so nice?
Śrīla Prabhupāda: No, rascaldom is not nice, but Kṛṣṇa is absolute. He is God. Therefore His rascaldom is also good. Kṛṣṇa is all-good. God is good.
Bob: Yes.
Śrīla Prabhupāda: Therefore, when He becomes a rascal, that is also good. Rascaldom is not good, but when it is practised by Kṛṣṇa that rascaldom is also good, because He is absolutely good. This one has to understand.
Bob: Are there some people who do not find Kṛṣṇa attractive?
Śrīla Prabhupāda: No. All people will find Him attractive. Who is not attracted? Just give an example: 'This man or this living entity is not attracted to Kṛṣṇa.' Just find such a person.

Bob: Somebody who wishes to do things in life that he may feel are wrong but who wishes to gain power or prestige or money may find God unattractive. He may not find God attractive, because God gives him guilt.

Śrīla Prabhupāda: No, not God. His attraction is to become powerful. A man wants to become powerful or rich—is it not? But nobody is richer than Kṛṣṇa. Therefore Kṛṣṇa is attractive to him.

Bob: If a person who wants to become rich prays to Kṛṣṇa, will he become rich?

Śrīla Prabhupāda: Oh, yes. Because Kṛṣṇa is all-powerful, if you pray to Kṛṣṇa to become rich, Kṛṣṇa will make you rich.

Bob: If somebody lives an evil life but prays to become rich, he may still become rich?

Śrīla Prabhupāda: Yes. Praying to Kṛṣṇa is not evil. [*Chuckling*] Somehow or other he prays to Kṛṣṇa, so you cannot say that he is evil.

Bob: Yes.

Śrīla Prabhupāda: Kṛṣṇa says in the *Bhagavad-gītā, api cet sudurācāro bhajate mām ananya-bhāk sādhur eva sa mantavyaḥ.* Have you read it?

Bob: Yes. The Sanskrit I don't know, but the English I do.

Śrīla Prabhupāda: Hmm.

Bob: 'Even if the most evil man prays to Me, he will be elevated.'

Śrīla Prabhupāda: Yes. As soon as he begins to pray to Kṛṣṇa, that is not evil. Therefore Kṛṣṇa is all-attractive. It is said in the *Vedas* that the Absolute Truth, or the Supreme Personality of Godhead, is the reservoir of all pleasure—*raso vai saḥ.* Everyone is hankering after someone because he realizes some mellow in it.

Bob: Excuse me?

Śrīla Prabhupāda: Some mellow. Suppose a man is drinking. Why is he drinking? He is getting some mellow out of that drinking. A man is hankering after money because by possessing money he gets a mellow out of it.

Bob: What does mellow mean?

Śrīla Prabhupāda: [*to Śyāmasundara*] How do they define mellow?

Śyāmasundara: Taste, pleasure.

Bob: OK.

Śrīla Prabhupāda: Pleasing taste. So the *Vedas* say, *raso vai saḥ*. The exact translation of mellow is *rasa*. [*Mālatī, Śyāmasundara's wife, enters with a tray of food.*] What is that?

Mālatī: Eggplant, fried.

Śrīla Prabhupāda: Oh! All-attractive! All-attractive! [*Laughter.*]

Bob: What is a scientist?

Śrīla Prabhupāda: One who knows things as they are.

Bob: He *thinks* he knows things as they are.

Śrīla Prabhupāda: What?

Bob: He *hopes* he knows things as they are.

Śrīla Prabhupāda: No, he is supposed to know. We approach the scientist because he is supposed to know things correctly. A scientist means one who knows things as they are.

Śyāmasundara: How is Kṛṣṇa the greatest scientist?

Śrīla Prabhupāda: Because He knows everything. A scientist is one who knows a subject matter thoroughly. Kṛṣṇa knows everything, so He is the greatest scientist.

Bob: I am presently a science teacher.

Śrīla Prabhupāda: Yes, but unless you have perfect knowledge, how can you teach? That is our question.

Bob: Without perfect knowledge, though, you can teach…

Śrīla Prabhupāda: That is cheating; that is not teaching. That is cheating. The scientists say, 'There was a chunk, and the creation took place. Perhaps. Maybe.' What is this? Simply cheating! It is not teaching; it is cheating.

Bob: Without perfect knowledge, can I not teach some things? For example, I may…

Śrīla Prabhupāda: You can teach up to the point you know.

Bob: Yes, but I should not claim to teach more than I know.

Śrīla Prabhupāda: Yes, that is cheating.

Śyāmasundara: In other words, he can't teach the truth with partial knowledge.

Śrīla Prabhupāda: Yes. That is not possible for any human being. A human being has imperfect senses. So how can he teach perfect knowledge? Suppose you see the sun as a disc. You have no means to approach the sun. If you say that we can see the sun by telescope and this and that, they are also made by you, and you are imperfect. So how can your machine be perfect? Therefore, your knowledge of the sun is imperfect. So don't teach about the sun unless you have perfect knowledge. That is cheating.

Bob: But what about teaching that it is supposed that the sun is 93,000,000 miles away?

Śrīla Prabhupāda: As soon as you say 'it is supposed,' it is not scientific.

Bob: But I think that almost all science, then, is not scientific.

Śrīla Prabhupāda: That is the point!

Bob: All science is based on, you know, suppositions of this or that.

Śrīla Prabhupāda: Yes. They are teaching imperfectly. Just like they are advertising so much about the moon. Do you think their knowledge is perfect?

Bob: No.

Śrīla Prabhupāda: Then?

Bob: What is the proper duty of the teacher in society? Let us say a science teacher. What should he be doing in the classroom?

Śrīla Prabhupāda: Classroom? You should simply teach about Kṛṣṇa.

Bob: He should not teach about…

Śrīla Prabhupāda: No. That will include everything. His aim should be to know Kṛṣṇa.

Bob: Can a scientist teach the science of combining acid and alkali —this kind of science—with Kṛṣṇa as its object?

Śrīla Prabhupāda: How can it be?

Bob: When one studies science, one finds general tendencies of nature, and these general tendencies of nature point to a controlling force…

Śrīla Prabhupāda: That I was explaining the other day. I asked a chemist whether, according to chemical formulas, hydrogen and oxygen linked together become water. Do they not?

Bob: It's true.

Śrīla Prabhupāda: Now, there is a vast amount of water in the Atlantic Ocean and Pacific Ocean. What quantity of chemicals was required?

Bob: How much?

Śrīla Prabhupāda: Yes. How many tons?

Bob: Many!

Śrīla Prabhupāda: So who supplied it?

Bob: This was supplied by God.

Śrīla Prabhupāda: Somebody must have supplied it.

Bob: Yes.

Śrīla Prabhupāda: So that is science. You can teach like that.

Bob: Should one bother teaching that if you combine acid and alkali they form a neutral?

Śrīla Prabhupāda: The same thing. There are so many effervescences. So, who is making them? Who is supplying the acid and alkali?

Bob: They come from the same source as the water.

Śrīla Prabhupāda: Yes. You cannot manufacture water unless you have hydrogen and oxygen. So, there are vast oceans—not only this Atlantic and Pacific: there are millions of planets, and there are millions of Atlantic and Pacific oceans. So who created this water with hydrogen and oxygen, and how was it supplied? That is our question. Somebody must have supplied it; otherwise how has it come into existence?

Bob: But should it also be taught how you make water from hydrogen and oxygen? The procedure of bringing them together—should this also be taught?

Śrīla Prabhupāda: That is secondary. That is not very difficult. Just like Mālatī made this *purī* [a kind of bread]. So, there is flour, and there is ghee [clarified butter], and she made a *purī*. But unless there is ghee and flour, where is the chance of making a *purī*? In the *Bhagavad-gītā* Kṛṣṇa makes this statement: 'Water, earth, air, fire—they are My energies.' What is your body? This external body—that is your energy. Do you know that? Your body is made out of your energy. For example, I am eating…

Bob: Yes.

Śrīla Prabhupāda: So I am creating some energy, and therefore my body is maintained.

Bob: Oh, I see.

Śrīla Prabhupāda: So therefore your body is made out of your energy.

Bob: But when you eat the food, there is energy from the sun in the food.

Śrīla Prabhupāda: So, I am giving an example. I am creating some energy by digesting the food, and that is maintaining my body. If your energy supply is not proper, then your body becomes weak or unhealthy. Your body is made out of your own energy. Similarly, this gigantic cosmic body—the universe—is made of Kṛṣṇa's energy. How can you deny it? As your body is made out of your energy, so the universal body must be made by somebody's energy. That is Kṛṣṇa.

Bob: I'll have to think about it to follow that.

Śrīla Prabhupāda: What is to follow? It is a fact. [*He laughs.*] Your hair is growing daily. Why? Because you have some energy.

Bob: The energy I obtain from my food.

Śrīla Prabhupāda: Somehow or other you have obtained that energy! And through that energy your hair is growing. So if your body is manufactured by your energy, similarly the whole gigantic manifestation is made of God's energy. It is a fact! It is not *your* energy.

Bob: Yes. Oh, I see that.

A devotee: Just like—aren't the planets in this universe the sun's energy—a product of the sun's energy?

Śrīla Prabhupāda: Yes, but who produced the sun? That is Kṛṣṇa's energy. The sun is simply heat, and Kṛṣṇa says, *bhūmir āpo 'nalo vāyuḥ: 'Anala*—heat—that is My energy.' The sun is the representation of the heating energy of Kṛṣṇa. It is not your energy. You cannot say, 'The sun is made by me.' But somebody must have made it, and Kṛṣṇa says that He did. So, we believe Kṛṣṇa. Therefore we are Kṛṣṇa-ites.

Bob: Kṛṣṇa-ites?

Śrīla Prabhupāda: Yes. And therefore our knowledge is perfect. If I say that heat is the energy of Kṛṣṇa, you cannot deny it, because it is not your energy. In your body there is some certain amount of heat. Similarly, the sun's heat is someone's energy. And who is that person? That is Kṛṣṇa. Kṛṣṇa says, 'Yes, it is My energy.' So my knowledge is perfect. Because I take the version of the greatest scientist, I am the greatest scientist. I may be a fool personally, but because I take knowledge from the greatest scientist, I am the greatest scientist. I have no difficulty.

Bob: Excuse me?

Śrīla Prabhupāda: I have no difficulty in becoming the greatest scientist because I take knowledge from the greatest scientist. We accept what Kṛṣṇa says in the *Bhagavad-gītā,* 'This earth, water, fire, air, ether, mind, intelligence, and ego—they are My eight separated energies.'

Bob: They are *separated* energies?

Śrīla Prabhupāda: Yes. Just like this milk. What is this milk? The separated energy of the cow. [*Śyāmasundara and Bob, stunned, laugh in realization.*] Is it not? It is the manifestation of the separated energy of the cow.

Śyāmasundara: Is it like a by-product?

Śrīla Prabhupāda: Yes.

Bob: So, what is the significance of this energy's being separated from Kṛṣṇa?

Śrīla Prabhupāda: 'Separated' means that this is made out of the body of the cow but it is not the cow. That is separation.

Bob: So, this earth and all is made out of Kṛṣṇa but it is not Kṛṣṇa?

Śrīla Prabhupāda: It is not Kṛṣṇa. Or, you can say it is Kṛṣṇa and not Kṛṣṇa simultaneously. That is our philosophy—one and different.

You cannot say that the things of this world are different from Kṛṣṇa, because without Kṛṣṇa they have no existence. At the same time, you cannot say, 'Then let me worship water. Why worship Kṛṣṇa?' The pantheists say that because everything is God, whatever we do is God worship. This is Māyāvāda philosophy—that because everything is made of God's energy, therefore everything is God. But our philosophy is that everything is God but also not God.

Bob: Is there anything on earth that is God?

Śrīla Prabhupāda: Yes. In one sense everything here is God because everything is made out of the energy of God. But that does not mean that by worshipping anything you are worshipping God.

Bob: So what is on earth that is not *māyā* [illusion]?

Śrīla Prabhupāda: *Māyā* means 'energy.'

Bob: It means energy?

Śrīla Prabhupāda: Yes. And another meaning of *māyā* is 'illusion.' So foolish persons accept the energy as the energetic. That is *māyā*. Suppose the sunshine enters your room. Sunshine is the energy of the sun, but simply because the sunshine enters your room you cannot say that the sun has entered. If the sun itself enters your room, then your room and yourself—everything—will be finished. Immediately. You will not have the leisure to understand that the sun has entered. Is it not?

Bob: It is so.

Śrīla Prabhupāda: Still, you cannot say that sunshine is not the sun. Without the sun, where is the sunshine? But at the same time, it is not the sun. It is the sun and not the sun—both. That is our philosophy. *Acintya-bhedābheda*—inconceivable difference and non-difference. In the material sense, you cannot conceive that a thing is simultaneously positive and negative. But that is the spiritual reality. And because everything is Kṛṣṇa's energy, Kṛṣṇa can manifest Himself from any energy. Therefore, when we worship Kṛṣṇa in a form made of something—of earth, stone, metal, or something like that—that is Kṛṣṇa. You cannot say that it is not

Kṛṣṇa. When we worship this metal form of Kṛṣṇa [the Deity form in the temple], that is Kṛṣṇa. That's a fact, because metal is an energy of Kṛṣṇa's. Therefore, it is nondifferent from Kṛṣṇa. And Kṛṣṇa is so powerful that He can present Himself fully in His energy. So this Deity worship is not heathenism. It is actually worship of God, provided you know the process.

Bob: If you know the process, then the Deity becomes Kṛṣṇa?

Śrīla Prabhupāda: Not becomes—it *is* Kṛṣṇa.

Bob: The Deity is Kṛṣṇa, but only if you know the process?

Śrīla Prabhupāda: Yes. Just like this electric wire—it is electricity. One who knows the process can derive electricity out of it.

Śyāmasundara: Otherwise it's just wire.

Śrīla Prabhupāda: Just wire.

Bob: So if I build a statue of Kṛṣṇa, it is not Kṛṣṇa unless…

Śrīla Prabhupāda: It is Kṛṣṇa. But you have to know the process of understanding that it is Kṛṣṇa. It is Kṛṣṇa.

Bob: It is not just earth and mud.

Śrīla Prabhupāda: No. Earth has no separate existence without Kṛṣṇa. Kṛṣṇa says, 'Earth is My energy.' You cannot separate the energy from the energetic. It is not possible. You cannot separate heat from fire. Still, fire is different from the heat, and heat is different from the fire. You are feeling heat; that does not mean you are touching fire. Fire, in spite of emanating heat, keeps its identity.

Similarly, although Kṛṣṇa, by His different energies, is creating everything, He remains Kṛṣṇa. The Māyāvādī philosophers think that if Kṛṣṇa is everything, then Kṛṣṇa's separate identity is lost. That is material thinking. For example, by my drinking this milk, little by little, when I finish there is no more milk; it has gone to my belly. Kṛṣṇa is not like that. He is omnipotent. We are utilizing His energy continually; still He is there, present.

A crude example: a man begets many children, but the man is still there. It's not that because he has produced many children he is finished. Similarly, God, or Kṛṣṇa, in spite of His unlimited number of children, is still there. *Pūrṇasya pūrṇam ādāya pūrṇam evāvaśiṣyate:* 'Because He is the Complete Whole, even though so many complete units emanate from Him, He remains the complete balance.' This is Kṛṣṇa consciousness. Kṛṣṇa is never finished. Kṛṣṇa is so powerful. Therefore He is all-attractive. This is one side of the display of Kṛṣṇa's energy. Similarly, He has unlimited energies. This study of Kṛṣṇa's energy is only one side, or a portion only. So in this way, if you go on studying Kṛṣṇa, that is Kṛṣṇa consciousness. It is not a bogus thing—'maybe,' 'perhaps not.' Absolutely! It is!

Śyāmasundara: And the study itself is never finished.

Śrīla Prabhupāda: No. How can it be? Kṛṣṇa has unlimited energy.

TWO

Vedic Culture: Varṇāśrama-dharma

Māyāpur, India—February 28, 1972

Bob: I've asked devotees about how they feel toward sex in their relations, and I see the way they feel, but I can't see myself acting the same way. See, I'll be getting married at the end of this summer.

Śrīla Prabhupāda: Hmm?

Bob: I'll be getting married at the end of this summer, in September or August when I return to America. And the devotees say that the householders only have sex to conceive a child, and I cannot picture myself at all in such a position. What kind of sex life can a devotee lead, living in the material world?

Śrīla Prabhupāda: The Vedic principle is that one should avoid sex life altogether. The whole Vedic principle is to get liberation from material bondage. There are different attachments for material enjoyment, of which sex life is the topmost. The *Bhāgavatam* says that in this material world man is attached to woman, and woman is attached to man: *puṁsaḥ striyā mithunī-bhāvam etam.* Not only in human society—in animal society also. That attachment is the basic principle of material life. So, a woman is hankering for or seeking after the association of a man, and a man is hankering for or seeking the association of a woman. All the fiction novels, dramas, cinemas, and even ordinary advertisements that you see simply depict the attachment between man and woman. Even in the tailor's shop you will find in the window some woman and some man. So this attachment is already there.

Bob: Attachment between man and woman?

Śrila Prabhupāda: Yes. So if you want to get liberation from this material world, then that attachment should be reduced to nil. Otherwise, simply further attachment. You will have to take rebirth, either as a human being or as a demigod or as an animal, as a serpent, as a bird, as a beast. You will have to take birth.

So, this basic principle of increasing attachment is not our business, although it is the general tendency. *Gṛha, kṣetra, suta* [home, land, children]. But if one can reduce and stop it, that is first class. Therefore our Vedic system is to first of all train a boy as a *brahmacārī*—no sex life. The Vedic principle is to reduce attachment, not to increase it. Therefore the whole system is called *varṇāśrama-dharma.*

The Indian system calls for *varṇa* and *āśrama*—four social orders and four spiritual orders. *Brahmacarya* [celibate student life], *gṛhastha* [married life], *vānaprastha* [retired life], and *sannyāsa* [renounced life]—these are the spiritual orders. And the social orders consist of *brāhmaṇas* [intellectuals], *kṣatriyas* [administrators], *vaiśyas* [merchants and farmers], and *śūdras* [ordinary workers]. So under this system, the regulative principles are so nice that even if one has the tendency to enjoy material life, he is so nicely moulded that at last he achieves liberation and goes back home, back to Godhead. This is the process. So sex life is not required, but because we are attached to it, there are some regulative principles under which it is maintained.

[*Chanting starts somewhere in the background, with exotic* mṛdaṅga *drumbeats amidst laughing and the loud blowing of horns.*]

It is said in *Śrīmad-Bhāgavatam* [5.5.8]:

puṁsaḥ striyā mithunī-bhāvam etaṁ
tayor mitho hṛdaya-granthim āhuḥ
ato gṛha-kṣetra-sutāpta-vittair
janasya moho 'yam ahaṁ mameti

This sex life is the basic principle of material life—attachment for man or woman. And when a man and woman are united, that attachment becomes increased, and that increased attachment will induce one to accumulate *gṛha* (a home), *kṣetra* (land), *suta* (children), *āpta* (friendship or society), and *vitta,* money. In this way—*gṛha-kṣetra-sutāpta-vittaiḥ*—he becomes entangled. *Janasya moho 'yam:* this is illusion. And by this illusion he thinks, *ahaṁ mameti:* 'I am this body, and anything in relationship with this body is mine.'
Bob: What is that again?
Śrīla Prabhupāda: The attachment increases. The material attachment involves thinking 'I am this body, and because I have this body in this particular place, this is my country.' And that is going on: 'I am American, I am Indian, I am German, I am this, I am that. This is my country. I shall sacrifice everything for my country and society.' So in this way, the illusion increases. And under this illusion, when he dies he gets another body. It may be a superior body or an inferior body, according to his *karma.* So if he gets a superior body, then that is also an entanglement, even if he goes to the heavenly planets. But if he becomes a cat or dog, then his life is lost. Or a tree—there is every chance of it.

So this science is not known in the world—how the soul is transmigrating from one body to another, and how he is being entrapped in different types of bodies. This science is unknown. In the *Bhagavad-gītā* Arjuna lamented, 'How can I kill my brother or my grandfather on the other side?' He was simply thinking on the basis of the bodily concept of life. But when he could not solve his problems, he surrendered to Kṛṣṇa and accepted Him as spiritual master. And when Kṛṣṇa became his spiritual master, He chastised Arjuna in the beginning [Bg. 2.11]:

aśocyān anvaśocas tvaṁ
prajñā-vādāṁś ca bhāṣase
gatāsūn agatāsūṁś ca
nānuśocanti paṇḍitāḥ

'You are talking like a learned man, but you are fool number one because you are talking about the bodily concept of life.' So sex life increases the bodily concept of life. Therefore, the whole process is to reduce it to nil.

Bob: To reduce it over the stages of your life?

Śrīla Prabhupāda: Yes. Reduce it. A boy is trained as a student up to age twenty-five, restricting sex life. *Brahmacārī.* So, some of the boys remain *naiṣṭhika-brahmacārī* [celibate for life]. Because they are given an education and they become fully conversant with spiritual knowledge, they don't want to marry. And even if they do marry, sex life is restricted. But the basic principle is that one cannot have sex life without being married. Therefore in human society there is marriage, not in animal society.

But people are gradually descending from human society to animal society. They are forgetting marriage. That is also predicted in the *śāstras* [scriptures]. *Dāmpatye 'bhirucir hetuḥ:* in the Kali-yuga [the present age of quarrel], eventually there will be no marriage; the boy and the girl will simply agree to live together, and their relationship will exist on sexual power. If the man or the woman is deficient in sex life, then there is divorce. So, for this philosophy there are many Western philosophers like Freud and others who have written so many books. But according to Vedic culture, we are interested in sex only for begetting children, that's all. Not to study the psychology of sex life. There is already natural psychology for that. Even if one does not read any philosophy, he is sexually inclined. Nobody is taught it in the schools and colleges. Everyone already knows how to do it. [*He laughs.*] That is the general tendency. But education should be given to *stop* it. That is real education.

Bob: In America at present that's a radical concept.

Śrīla Prabhupāda: Well, in America there are so many things that require reformation, and this Kṛṣṇa consciousness movement will bring that. I went to your country and saw that the boys and girls were living like friends, so I said to my students, 'You cannot live together as friends; you must get yourselves married.'

Bob: Many people see that even marriage is not sacred, so they find no desire to marry. They see that often people get married, and if things are not proper they get a divorce so very easily. Therefore many people feel that to get married is not meaningful.

Śrīla Prabhupāda: Their idea is that marriage is for legalized prostitution. They think like that, but that is not marriage. Even that Christian paper—what is that?

Śyāmasundara: *Watchtower.*

Śrīla Prabhupāda: *Watchtower.* It has criticized that one priest has allowed a marriage between two men—homosexuality. So these things are all going on. People are taking to marriage purely for prostitution, that's all. So therefore people are thinking, 'What is the use of keeping a regular prostitute at such heavy expenditure? Better not to have this.'

Śyāmasundara: You use that example of the cow and the market.

Śrīla Prabhupāda: Yes. When milk is available in the marketplace, what is the use of keeping a cow? [*Everyone laughs.*] It is a very abominable condition in the Western countries. I have seen it. Here also, in India, gradually it is coming. Therefore we have started this Kṛṣṇa consciousness movement to educate people in the essential principles of spiritual life. It is not a sectarian religious movement. It is a cultural movement for everyone's benefit.

THREE

The Real Goal of Life

Māyāpur, India—February 28, 1972 (continued)

Śrīla Prabhupāda: This movement is especially meant to enable a human being to reach the real goal of life.
Bob: Is the real goal of life to know God?
Śrīla Prabhupāda: Yes. To go back home, back to Godhead. That is the real goal of life. The water that comes from the sea forms clouds, the clouds fall down as rain, and the actual goal is to flow down the river and again enter the sea. So, we have come from God, and now we are embarrassed by material life. Therefore, our aim should be to get out of this embarrassing situation and go back home, back to Godhead. This is the real goal of life.

mām upetya punar janma
duḥkhālayam aśāśvatam
nāpnuvanti mahātmānaḥ
saṁsiddhiṁ paramāṁ gatāḥ

This is the version of *Bhagavad-gītā* [8.15]. Kṛṣṇa says, 'If anyone comes to Me, he does not come back again.' Where? 'To this place—*duḥkhālayam aśāśvatam.*' This place is the abode of miseries. Everyone knows it, but they have been befooled by so-called leaders. Material life is miserable life. Kṛṣṇa says, God says, that this place is *duḥkhālayam*—it is a place of miseries. And it is also *aśāśvatam,* temporary. You cannot make a compromise: 'All right, let it be miserable. I shall remain here as an American or Indian.' No. That also you cannot do. You cannot remain an American. You may think that, having been born in America, you are very happy. But you cannot remain an American for long. You will have to be kicked out of that place. And your next life you do not know! Therefore, it is *duḥkhālayam aśāśvatam*—miserable and temporary. That is our philosophy.

Bob: But when you have some knowledge of God, then life is not so miserable?

Śrīla Prabhupāda: No! *Some* knowledge will not do. You must have *perfect* knowledge. *Janma karma ca me divyam evaṁ yo vetti tattvataḥ. Tattvataḥ* means 'perfectly.' Perfect knowledge is being taught in the *Bhagavad-gītā.* So, we are giving everyone in human society a chance to learn the *Bhagavad-gītā* as it is and make his life perfect. That is the Kṛṣṇa consciousness movement. What does your science say about the transmigration of the soul?

Bob: I think that science cannot deny or affirm it. Science does not know it.

Śrīla Prabhupāda: Therefore I say that your science is imperfect.

Bob: Science may, though, say something. It is said in science that energy is never destroyed; it is changed.

Śrīla Prabhupāda: That's all right. But how is the energy working in the future—that science does not know. How is the energy diverted? How, by different manipulations, is the energy working differently? For instance, electrical energy. By different handling it is operating the heater and it is operating the refrigerator. They are just the opposite, but the electrical energy is the same. Similarly, this energy—living energy—how is it being directed? Which way is it going? How is it fructifying in the next life? That they do not know. But in the *Bhagavad-gītā* it is very simply stated, *vāsāṁsi jīrṇāni yathā vihāya:* You are covered by a shirt and coat. When this shirt and coat is unusable, you change it. Similarly, this body is just like a shirt and coat. When it is no longer workable, we have to change it.

Bob: What is the 'we' that has to change? What is constant?

Śrīla Prabhupāda: That is the soul.

Bob: From one life to the next?

Śrīla Prabhupāda: That is the soul—I. What 'you' is speaking? What 'I' is speaking? Identity: *ātmā,* or soul.

Bob: My soul is different from your soul?

Śrīla Prabhupāda: Yes. You are an individual soul, I am an individual soul.

Bob: You have removed yourself from karmic influences. If I were to remove myself from karmic influences, would our souls be the same or different?

Śrīla Prabhupāda: The soul is of the same quality in all. You are under a certain conception of life at the present moment, and these countrymen of yours [*gestures to the devotees present*] were under a certain conception of life, but by training they have taken to another conception of life. So the ultimate training is how to become Kṛṣṇa conscious. That is the perfection.

Bob: If two people are Kṛṣṇa conscious, is their soul the same?

Śrīla Prabhupāda: The soul is always the same.

Bob: In each person? In each person is it the same?

Śrīla Prabhupāda: Yes.

Bob: [*pointing to two devotees*] If these two are Kṛṣṇa conscious, are their souls the same?

Śrīla Prabhupāda: The soul is the same but always individual, even if one is not Kṛṣṇa conscious. For instance, you are a human being, and I am a human being. Even if I am not a Christian, even if you are not a Hindu, still we are human beings. Similarly, the soul may not be Kṛṣṇa conscious, or he may be Kṛṣṇa conscious—it doesn't matter. But the soul is the soul.

Bob: Can you tell me more about this?

Śrīla Prabhupāda: Soul—as pure spirit, all souls are equal. Even in an animal. Therefore it is said, *paṇḍitāḥ sama-darśinaḥ:* those who are actually learned do not see the outward covering, either in a human being or in an animal.

Bob: If I may ask another question on this?

Śrīla Prabhupāda: Yes.

Bob: I have considered the soul somewhat as part of God. At times I think I feel God. I'm here, and you may say God is here. So if the soul is inside me, then should I be able to feel God inside me? Not all of God, I mean, but a…

Śrīla Prabhupāda: Part of God.

Bob: But I don't feel God in me, but God may be here, separate—separate from me. But should I be able to feel God inside me, since my soul is part of God?

Śrīla Prabhupāda: Yes. God is inside also. God is everywhere. God is inside and outside also. This is to be known.

Bob: How do you feel God inside you?

Śrīla Prabhupāda: Not in the beginning, but you have to know from the *śāstras* [scriptures], by the Vedic information. For example, in the *Bhagavad-gītā* [18.61] it is said, *īśvaraḥ sarva-bhūtānāṁ hṛd-deśe 'rjuna tiṣṭhati:* God is there in everyone's heart. *Paramāṇu-cayāntara-stham:* God is also within every atom. So this is the first information. And then, by the yogic process, you have to realize it.

Bob: Yogic process?

Śrīla Prabhupāda: Yes.

Bob: Is chanting Hare Kṛṣṇa such a yogic process?

Śrīla Prabhupāda: Yes, it is also a yogic process.

Bob: What kind of yogic process must I do to find out—to feel this information—to feel the soul inside?

Śrīla Prabhupāda: Yes, there are many different yogic processes, but for this age this process is very nice.

Bob: Chanting.

Śrīla Prabhupāda: Yes.

Bob: Through this I can feel not only God outside but God inside?
Śrīla Prabhupāda: You'll understand everything of God—how God is inside, how God is outside, how God is working. Everything will be revealed. By this attitude of service, God will reveal Himself. You cannot understand God by your endeavour. Only if God reveals Himself. For instance, when the sun is out of your sight at night, you cannot see it by your torchlight, or any light. But in the morning you can see the sun automatically, without any torchlight. Similarly, you have to create a situation—you have to put yourself in a situation—in which God will be revealed. It is not that by some method you can order God, 'Come. I will see You.' No, God is not your order-carrier.
Bob: You must please God for Him to reveal Himself. Is that correct?
Śrīla Prabhupāda: Yes.
Śyāmasundara: How do we know when we are pleasing God?
Śrīla Prabhupāda: When we see Him. Then you will understand, just as when you eat you do not require to ask anyone whether you are feeling strength or your hunger is satisfied. If you eat, you understand that you are feeling energy. You don't need to inquire from anyone. Similarly, if you actually serve God, then you will understand, 'God is dictating to me. God is there. I am seeing God.'
Śyāmasundara: Or God's representative.
Śrīla Prabhupāda: Yes.
Śyāmasundara: It comes easier.
Śrīla Prabhupāda: You have to go through God's representative. *Yasya prasādād bhagavat-prasādaḥ:* If you please God's representative, then automatically God becomes pleased, and thus you can directly see Him.
Bob: How can we please God's representative?
Śrīla Prabhupāda: You have to carry out his orders, that's all. God's representative is the *guru.* He asks you to do this, to do that—if you do that, that is pleasing. *Yasyāprasādān na gatiḥ kuto 'pi:* If you displease the spiritual master, then you are nowhere. Therefore

we worship the *guru. Sākṣād-dharitvena samasta-śāstrair uktas tathā bhāvyata eva sadbhiḥ:* The *guru* should be accepted as God. That is the injunction of all *śāstra.*

Bob: The *guru* should be accepted as a representative of God?

Śrīla Prabhupāda: Yes, the *guru* is God's representative. The *guru* is the external manifestation of Kṛṣṇa.

Bob: But different from the incarnations of Kṛṣṇa that come?

Śrīla Prabhupāda: Yes.

Bob: In what way is the external manifestation of the *guru* different from the external manifestation of, let us say, Kṛṣṇa or Caitanya when They come to earth?

Śrīla Prabhupāda: The *guru* is the representative of Kṛṣṇa. So there are symptoms of who is a *guru.* The general symptoms are described in the *Vedas.*

tad-vijñānārthaṁ sa gurum evābhigacchet
samit-pāṇiḥ śrotriyaṁ brahma-niṣṭham

A *guru* must come in a disciplic succession, and he must have heard thoroughly about the *Vedas* from his spiritual master. Generally a *guru's* symptom is that he is a perfect devotee, that's all. And he serves Kṛṣṇa by preaching His message.

Bob: Lord Caitanya—He was a different type of *guru* than you are?

Śrīla Prabhupāda: No, no. *Gurus* cannot be of different types. All *gurus* are of one type.

Bob: But He was—was He also an incarnation at the same time?

Śrīla Prabhupāda: Yes, He is Kṛṣṇa Himself, but He is representing the *guru.*

Bob: I see.

Śrīla Prabhupāda: Because Kṛṣṇa was God, He demanded, *sarva-dharmān parityajya mām ekaṁ śaraṇaṁ vraja:* 'Abandon all varieties of religion and just surrender unto Me.' [Bg. 18.66] But people misunderstood Him. Therefore Kṛṣṇa again came as a *guru* and taught people *how* to surrender to Kṛṣṇa.

Śyāmasundara: Doesn't Kṛṣṇa say in *Bhagavad-gītā,* 'I am the spiritual master'?

Śrīla Prabhupāda: Yes, He is the original spiritual master because He was accepted as spiritual master by Arjuna. So what is the difficulty? Arjuna told the Lord, *śiṣyas te 'haṁ śādhi māṁ tvāṁ prapannam:* 'I am Your disciple, and a soul surrendered unto You. Please instruct me.' So unless Kṛṣṇa is a spiritual master, how does Arjuna become His disciple? Kṛṣṇa is the original *guru. Tene brahma hṛdā ya ādi-kavaye:* 'It is He only who first imparted Vedic knowledge unto the heart of Brahmā, the first created being.' Therefore He is the original *guru.*

Bob: Kṛṣṇa.

Śrīla Prabhupāda: Yes. He is the original *guru.* Then His disciple Brahmā is a *guru,* then Brahmā's disciple Nārada is a *guru,* then Nārada's disciple Vyāsa is a *guru*—in this way there is a *guru-paramparā,* a disciplic succession of *gurus. Evaṁ paramparā-prāptam:* the transcendental knowledge is received through the disciplic succession.

Bob: So a *guru* receives his knowledge through the disciplic succession, not directly from Kṛṣṇa? Do you receive some knowledge directly from Kṛṣṇa?

Śrīla Prabhupāda: Yes. Kṛṣṇa's direct instruction is there: *Bhagavad-gītā.*

Bob: I see, but…

Śrīla Prabhupāda: But you have to learn it through the disciplic succession; otherwise you will misunderstand it.

Bob: But presently you do not receive information directly from Kṛṣṇa? It comes through the disciplic succession from the books?

Śrīla Prabhupāda: There is no difference. Suppose I say that this is a pencil. If you say to him, 'This is a pencil,' and if he says to another man, 'This is a pencil,' then what is the difference between his instruction and my instructions?

Bob: Kṛṣṇa's mercy allows you to know this now?

Śrīla Prabhupāda: You can take Kṛṣṇa's mercy also, provided it is delivered as it is. Just as we are teaching the *Bhagavad-gītā.* In the *Bhagavad-gītā* [18.66] Kṛṣṇa says, *sarva-dharmān parityajya mām ekaṁ śaraṇaṁ vraja:* 'Just give up all other forms of religion and simply surrender unto Me.' Now, we are saying that you should give up everything and surrender to Kṛṣṇa. Therefore, there is no difference between Kṛṣṇa's instruction and our instruction. There is no deviation. So if you receive knowledge in that perfect way, that is as good as receiving instruction directly from Kṛṣṇa. But we don't change anything.

Bob: When I pray reverently, faithfully, does Kṛṣṇa hear me?

Śrīla Prabhupāda: Yes.

Bob: From me to Him?

Śrīla Prabhupāda: Yes, because He is within your heart He is always hearing you—whether you are praying or not praying. When you are doing some nonsense, He is also hearing you. And when you pray, that is very good—welcome.

Bob: To Kṛṣṇa's ear, is praying louder than nonsense?

Śrīla Prabhupāda: No. He is all-perfect. He can hear everything. Even if you don't speak, even if you simply think, 'I shall do it,' then He hears you. *Sarvasya cāhaṁ hṛdi sanniviṣṭaḥ:* Kṛṣṇa is seated in everyone's heart.

Bob: But one should pray—is that so?

Śrīla Prabhupāda: That is one's only business—praying.

Bob: Whose business?

Śrīla Prabhupāda: Every living entity's. That is the only business. *Eko bahūnāṁ yo vidadhāti kāmān.* That is the statement of the *Vedas.*

Bob: What does that mean?

Śrīla Prabhupāda: He supplies everything to everyone. He is supplying food to everyone. So He is the Father. So why should you not pray, 'Father, give me this'? Just as in the Christian Bible there is the prayer 'Father, give us our daily bread.' That is good—they are accepting the Supreme Father. But grown-up children should not ask from the father; rather, they should be prepared to serve the father. That is *bhakti,* devotion.

Bob: My questions you solve so nicely. [*Everyone laughs with affection.*]
Śrīla Prabhupāda: Thank you very much.
Bob: So, should I ask you another question now?
Śrīla Prabhupāda: Oh, yes. Yes!

FOUR

The Three Modes of Nature

Māyāpur, India—February 28, 1972 (continued)

Bob: I have read that in life there are three *guṇas*—passion, ignorance, and goodness. I was wishing that you would explain this somewhat, especially what is meant by the mode of ignorance and the mode of goodness.

Śrīla Prabhupāda: In goodness you can understand things—knowledge. You can know that there is God, that this world was created by Him, and so many things, actual things—the sun is this, the moon is this—perfect knowledge. If one has some knowledge, even though it may not be perfect, that is goodness. And in passion one identifies with his material body and tries to gratify his senses. That is passion. And ignorance is animal life—in ignorance, one does not know what is God, how to become happy, why we are in this world. For example, if you take an animal to the slaughterhouse, it will go willingly. This is ignorance. But a man will protest. If a goat is to be killed after five minutes but you give it a morsel of grass, it is happy because it is eating. That is ignorance.

Bob: Being in these modes determines your *karma*. Is that correct?

Śrīla Prabhupāda: Yes. According to the association of the modes of nature, your activities are being contaminated. *Kāraṇaṁ guṇa-saṅgo 'sya sad-asad-yoni-janmasu:* 'A man gets a higher birth or lower birth according to the association of the *guṇas,* or the modes of nature.' [Bg. 13.22]

Bob: So, cheating and things like that—what mode is that?

Śrīla Prabhupāda: Cheating is mixed passion and ignorance. Suppose one man cheats another. That means he wants to obtain something; he is passionate. But if he commits murder, he does not know that he will have to suffer for it. So it is a mixture of passion and ignorance.

Bob: And what about when somebody helps another person?

Śrīla Prabhupāda: That is goodness.

Bob: Why is that goodness? You said that goodness is when you have knowledge. So helping someone represents knowledge of what?

Śrīla Prabhupāda: If he is ignorant and you are trying to enlighten him, that is goodness.

Bob: So giving knowledge is goodness?

Śrīla Prabhupāda: Yes.

Bob: And what about just giving assistance?

Śrīla Prabhupāda: That is also goodness.

Bob: If a beggar has nothing and you give him alms…

Śrīla Prabhupāda: That may still be goodness. But in your Bowery Street, they give someone charity, and immediately he purchases a bottle of wine and drinks and lies down flat. [*All laugh.*] So that is charity, but that is not goodness; that is ignorance.

Bob: Charity can be ignorance?

Śrīla Prabhupāda: There are three kinds of charities—in goodness, passion, and ignorance. Charity in goodness means giving charity where charity must be given. Just like this Kṛṣṇa consciousness movement—if anyone gives charity to this movement, that is charity in goodness because it is spreading God consciousness, Kṛṣṇa consciousness. That is charity in goodness. And if one gives charity for some return, that is charity in passion. And if somebody gives charity at an improper place and time, without respect, and to an unworthy person, just like the Bowery man, that is charity in ignorance. But Kṛṣṇa says, *yat karoṣi yad aśnāsi yaj juhoṣi dadāsi yat:* 'Whatever you do, whatever you eat, whatever you offer or give away, and whatever austerities you perform—do that as an offering to Me.' [Bg. 9.27] If Kṛṣṇa takes your offering, that is the perfection of charity. Or anyone who is a representative of Kṛṣṇa—if he takes it, that is perfection.

Bob: And what kind of charity is it when you give food to somebody who is hungry?

Śrīla Prabhupāda: Well, that depends on the circumstances. For example, if a doctor has forbidden his patient to take any solid food, and if the patient is asking, 'Give me some solids,' and if you give him solid food in charity, then you are not doing good to him. That is ignorance.

Bob: Are the devotees beyond accumulating *karma*? These devotees—do they feel *karma*? Do they work in these modes? Are they in the mode of goodness?

Śrīla Prabhupāda: They are above goodness! *Śuddha-sattva.* The devotees are not in this material world. They are in the spiritual world. That is stated in the *Bhagavad-gītā* [14.26]:

māṁ ca yo 'vyabhicāreṇa
bhakti-yogena sevate
sa guṇān samatītyaitān
brahma-bhūyāya kalpate

['One who engages in full devotional service, unfailing in all circumstances, at once transcends the modes of material nature and thus comes to the level of Brahman.'] Devotees are neither in goodness, passion, nor ignorance. They are transcendental to all these qualities.

Bob: A devotee who is very faithful reaches this stage?

Śrīla Prabhupāda: Yes. You can become a devotee as they have become. It is not difficult. Simply you have to engage yourself in the transcendental loving service of the Lord, that's all.
Bob: What is the status of service minus devotion?
Śrīla Prabhupāda: Hmm? That is not service, that is business. [*Everyone laughs.*] For example, here in Māyāpur we have employed a contractor. That is not service—that is business. Is it not? Sometimes they will advertise, 'Our customers are our masters.' Is it not? But in spite of the flowery language—'Our customers are our masters'—this is business, because nobody is a qualified customer unless he pays. But service is not like that. Caitanya Mahāprabhu prays to Kṛṣṇa, *yathā tathā vā vidadhātu lampaṭo mat-prāṇa-nāthas tu sa eva nāparaḥ:* 'You do whatever You like, but still You are my worshipable Lord.' That is service. 'I don't ask any return from You.' That is service. When you expect some return, that is business.
Bob: I wish to gain more knowledge of God and be able to feel God's presence more. I feel life has little meaning without this.
Śrīla Prabhupāda: Yes! If you misuse this human form of life, then it is a great loss. Human life is a great chance given to the living entity to get out of the entanglement of material existence.
Bob: I feel thankful that I've been able to ask these questions.
Śrīla Prabhupāda: Yes, you can learn more and more. Questions and answers are required. They are beneficial to all. Sūta Gosvāmī says [SB 1.2.5]:

munayaḥ sādhu pṛṣṭo 'haṁ
bhavadbhir loka-maṅgalam
yat kṛtaḥ kṛṣṇa-sampraśno
yenātmā suprasīdati

['O sages, I have been justly questioned by you. Your questions are worthy because they relate to Lord Kṛṣṇa and so are relevant to the world's welfare. Only questions of this sort are capable of completely satisfying the self.'] So, questions about Kṛṣṇa are very good. When you discuss and hear about Kṛṣṇa, that is *loka-maṅgalam,* auspicious for everyone. Both the questions and the answers.

Bob: I am attracted to devotional life, but I still have my connections at home. Marriage is… I'm engaged.

Śrīla Prabhupāda: No, no. There are so many marriages [*indicates Śyāmasundara*]. He is married. Marriage is no barrier. I told you that there are four orders of spiritual life—*brahmacārī, gṛhastha, vānaprastha,* and *sannyāsa.* So after *brahmacārī* life, one can marry, although it is not obligatory. One may remain *naiṣṭhika-brahmacārī*—unmarried for his whole life. But a *brahmacārī* may marry. And after marriage, there is *vānaprastha* life. This means that one is a little aloof from family—the husband and wife live separately. At that time there is no sex life. Then when he is fully renounced, detached from family life, he takes *sannyāsa.*

Bob: Does the *sannyāsī* forget his wife completely then?

Śrīla Prabhupāda: Yes. Forgetting is not very difficult, if you try to forget. Out of sight, out of mind. [*All laugh.*] Just as I have my wife, children, grandchildren—everything. But, out of sight, out of mind, that's all. Therefore, *vānaprastha, sannyāsa*—everything is nicely arranged by the Vedic system.

FIVE

Becoming Pure

Māyāpur, India—February 29, 1972

Bob: Thank you so much for allowing me to ask my questions.
Śrīla Prabhupāda: That is my mission. People should understand the science of God. Unless we cooperate with the Supreme Lord, our life is baffled. I have given the example many times that a screw which has fallen from a machine has no value, but when the same screw is again attached to the machine, it has value. Similarly, we are part and parcel of God. So without God, what is our value? No value! We should again come back to our position of attachment to God. Then we have value.
Bob: I met a young fellow today who came here because he heard that hippies were in Māyāpur.
Śrīla Prabhupāda: He's Indian?
Bob: Yes. He lives nearby and speaks English fairly well. When he was young he worshiped Kālī [a popular demigoddess] every day very rigorously. But when the floods came and the people saw hardship, he lost faith and now he has no religion. He said he now finds his happiness in trying to develop love among people. I couldn't think of what to say to him to add God and religion to his

life. He said that after he dies 'maybe I'll become part of God, maybe not,' but he can't worry about it now. He said he's tried various religious experiences, but they didn't work. One reason I ask this is because when I go back to America, a lot of people I come across are like this. They see that religion, like his worship of Kālī or other kinds of religion they've experienced, doesn't work. And I don't know what to say to them to convince them it's worth trying.

Śrīla Prabhupāda: Do not try at the present moment. *You* first of all become convinced, and then try to convince others. Caitanya Mahāprabhu's instruction is that you can improve the welfare of others when your own life is a success:

bhārata-bhūmite haila manuṣya-janma yāra
janma sārthaka kari' kara para-upakāra

First make your life perfect. Then try to teach others.

Bob: The devotees have told me that without consciousness of Kṛṣṇa all the time, you cannot be happy. But at times I feel happy.

Śrīla Prabhupāda: At times. Not always.

Bob: Yes.

Śrīla Prabhupāda: But if you become Kṛṣṇa conscious, you will feel happy always.

Bob: They implied that you cannot feel happy without Kṛṣṇa consciousness.

Śrīla Prabhupāda: That is a fact. For example, if you are an animal of the land and you are thrown into the water, you cannot be happy in the water in any condition. When you are again taken up on the land, then you'll be happy. Similarly, since we are part and parcel of Kṛṣṇa, we cannot be happy without acting as part and parcel of Kṛṣṇa. The same example as before: the machine part, fallen out of the machine, has no value, but when it is again put into the machine it has value. We are part of Kṛṣṇa; we must join Kṛṣṇa. And you can join Kṛṣṇa immediately by your consciousness, simply by thinking 'I am Kṛṣṇa's, Kṛṣṇa is mine.' That's all.

Bob: We are part of Kṛṣṇa.
Śrīla Prabhupāda: Yes. Everything is part and parcel of Kṛṣṇa because everything is generated by the energy of Kṛṣṇa and everything *is* the energy of Kṛṣṇa.
Bob: How I can come to feel closer to God? I come to the temple at times, and then I leave, and I'm not sure how much I take with me.
Śrīla Prabhupāda: You have to be purified. It does not take much time. Within six months you will realize your progress. But you have to follow the regulative principles, just as these boys and girls are doing. Then it will be all right.
Bob: Yes, I see.
Śrīla Prabhupāda: They have no tendency for going to the cinema or a nightclub. No. They have stopped all *anarthas,* all unnecessary things. The whole human life is meant for purification.

tapo divyaṁ putrakā yena sattvaṁ
śuddhyed yasmād brahma-saukhyaṁ tv anantam

Lord Ṛṣabhadeva says here that we should perform austerities and penances so that we can purify our existence (*sattva* means existence) and come to the stage of endless transcendental happiness. So if you don't purify your existence, then you will have to change your body from this to that. Sometimes it may be higher, sometimes lower. For example, if you don't cure a disease, it can put you into trouble in so many ways. Similarly, if you don't purify your existence, you will have to transmigrate from one body to another, and there is no guarantee you will get a very comfortable American body. Therefore, it is essential for a human being to purify his existence. Unless you purify your existence, you will hanker after happiness but will not always be happy.
Bob: When I go to my job in New York, I hope I'll become pure, but I'm sure that I won't become as pure as your devotees here. I don't see myself doing that.
Śrīla Prabhupāda: You can do as they are doing. They were not pure

in the beginning; now they are pure. Similarly, you can become pure. For example, in your childhood you were not educated, but now you are educated. If you are serious you can keep yourself pure anywhere. It doesn't matter whether you stay in America or India. But you must know how to keep yourself pure. That's all.

Bob: You mean by following the principles of Kṛṣṇa consciousness?

Śrīla Prabhupāda: Yes. I went to America, for instance, but whether in America or India, I am the same man.

Bob: I have somewhat tried to follow since I met you the first time last November.

Śrīla Prabhupāda: Hmm. But you must strictly follow if you are serious.

Bob: OK, maybe… What I will say now is—well—the most foolish of all I've said. But let me tell you how I feel.

Śrīla Prabhupāda: No, no, not foolish. I don't say you are foolish—but imperfect.

Bob: OK. [*He laughs.*] Imperfect. But let me tell you. I feel that right now I admire and respect your devotees, but I don't feel as if I am part of them, or even that I have a great desire to be part of them. I feel that I just want—I want to do what is right, come closer to God, and if I can just go to a better life next time, I'd be satisfied.

Śrīla Prabhupāda: Very good.

Bob: I guess it's material clinging, but…

Śrīla Prabhupāda: So, you just follow in their footsteps, and your desire will be fulfilled. We are training people how to become purified and happy. That is our mission: we want to see everyone happy. *Sarve sukhino bhavantu.* People do not know how to become happy. They do not take the standard path to become happy. They manufacture their own way. That is the difficulty. Therefore, Ṛṣabhadeva gave this advice to his sons: 'My dear boys, just undergo austerity for transcendental realization.' Everyone is performing austerity. One boy I know—he had to go to a foreign country to learn commercial management. Now he is well situated. In this way, everyone is undergoing some austerity for temporary material happiness. So why not undergo austerity for *permanent* happiness?

You have to purify your existence and your body. As many times as you accept a material body, you will have to change it. But as soon as you get a spiritual body, there is no question of change. You already have a spiritual body. Now, due to our material contamination, we are developing the material body. But if we associate with spiritual life, then we shall develop a spiritual body. If you put an iron rod within fire, it will become like fire. Is it not?

Bob: Yes.

Śrīla Prabhupada: And when the iron rod is red-hot, you can touch it anywhere, and it will burn. It takes on the quality of fire, although it is still iron. Similarly, if you always keep yourself in Kṛṣṇa consciousness, your body will become spiritualized and act spiritually, although it is material. No more material demands.

Bob: How do I do this?

Śrīla Prabhupāda: By the process we are teaching. You have seen these six boys who were initiated today. They are doing it; it is very simple. You have to follow the four restrictive regulations and chant Hare Kṛṣṇa on these beads. Very easy.

Bob: Well, but, I follow some of the regulative principles, but not all.

Śrīla Prabhupāda: 'Some' means? There are only four regulative principles. 'Some' means three, or two?

Bob: Two or three.

Śrīla Prabhupāda: So why not the other one?

Bob: No, no. I mean I follow one or two. One or two I follow now.

Śrīla Prabhupāda: [*Laughs.*] Why not the other three? What is the difficulty? Which one do you follow?

Bob: Well, I'm almost vegetarian, but I eat eggs.

Śrīla Prabhupāda: Then that is also not complete.

Bob: No. Since I saw you last November, I've become vegetarian.

Śrīla Prabhupāda: Vegetarian is no qualification. The pigeon is vegetarian. The monkey is vegetarian—the most rubbish creature, most mischievous.

Bob: I felt that it was a little bit of progress because it was somewhat difficult at first, then easy.

Śrīla Prabhupāda: No, you can stick to all the regulative principles, provided you take to the Kṛṣṇa consciousness process. Otherwise it is not possible.

Bob: Yes. When I'm back in Bihar with my friends and we're sitting in the evening and there's nothing to do but fight mosquitoes, they say, 'How about smoking some marijuana?' And I say, 'Sure, there's nothing else to do,' and then I sit down, and I enjoy myself for the evening. We were doing this every day—we got carried away—until we realized we were hurting ourselves and stopped. But still on occasion we…

Śrīla Prabhupāda: You have to live with *us.* Then your friends will not ask you, 'What about marijuana?' [*Bob laughs.*] Keep the association of devotees. We are opening centers to give people a chance to associate with us. Why have we bought so much land in Māyāpur? So that those who are seriously desirous of advancing in Kṛṣṇa consciousness can come live with us. Association is very influential. If you associate with drunkards, you become a drunkard; if you associate with *sādhus,* you become a *sādhu.*

Śyāmasundara: He can come and stay with you in Bombay.

Śrīla Prabhupāda: Yes, you can stay with us in Bombay. But he wants friends with marijuana. That is the difficulty.

Bob: Let me ask you about something else; then maybe I'll come back to this. I find that I think of myself too much, and this way I can't think of God so much. I think of myself in too many places. How can I forget about myself so I can concentrate on other, more important things?

Śrīla Prabhupāda: As these devotees have done.

Bob: [*Laughs.*] I think what you're saying to me is that my path to purity is to become a devotee.

Śrīla Prabhupāda: Do you hesitate?

Bob: Well, I…

Śrīla Prabhupāda: Is it very difficult to become a devotee?

Bob: For me it is. I don't feel so much the desire. First the devotees tell me that they have given up material life. These four regulative principles, they have explained to me, mean giving up material life, and that I see. And in place of this they have…

Śrīla Prabhupāda: What do you mean by material life? [*Bob is silent.*] I am sitting on this bed. Is it material or spiritual?

Bob: Material.

Śrīla Prabhupāda: Then how have we given up material life?

Bob: I think how I interpreted it was 'a desire for material gain.'

Śrīla Prabhupāda: What is material?

Bob: Working toward material gain and not giving up all material desires.

Śrīla Prabhupāda: When you desire to gratify your senses, that is material life. And when you desire to serve God, that is spiritual life. That is the difference between material life and spiritual life. Now we are trying to serve our senses. But instead of serving our senses we should serve God; that is spiritual life. What is the difference between our activities and others'? We are using everything they use—table, chair, bed, tape recorder, typewriter—so what is the difference? The difference is that we are using everything for Kṛṣṇa.

Bob: The devotees have said that the sensual pleasures they have given up are replaced with spiritual kinds of pleasures, but I haven't felt this.

Śrīla Prabhupāda: Spiritual pleasures come when you desire to please Kṛṣṇa. That is spiritual pleasure. For example, a mother is more pleased by feeding her son. She's not eating, but when she sees that her son is eating very nicely, then she becomes pleased.

Bob: Hmm. Spiritual pleasure, then, is pleasing God.

Śrīla Prabhupāda: Spiritual pleasure means the pleasure of Kṛṣṇa.

Bob: Pleasing Kṛṣṇa.

Śrīla Prabhupāda: Yes. Material pleasure means the pleasure of the senses. That's all. This is the difference. When you simply try to please Kṛṣṇa, that is spiritual pleasure.

Bob: My thought of pleasing God was to…

Śrīla Prabhupāda: Don't manufacture your own ways of pleasing God. Suppose I want to please you. Then I shall ask you, 'How can I serve you?' Not that I manufacture some service. That is not pleasing. Suppose I want a glass of water. If you concoct the idea, 'Swamiji will be more pleased if I give him a glass of hot milk,' that will not please me. If you want to please me, then you should ask me, 'How can I please you?' And if you do what I order, that will please me.

Bob: And pleasing Kṛṣṇa, then, is being a devotee of Kṛṣṇa.

Śrīla Prabhupāda: A devotee is one who is always pleasing Kṛṣṇa. He has no other business. That is a devotee.

Bob: Can you tell me some more about chanting Hare Kṛṣṇa? I have for quite some time chanted, but never regularly—just a little bit here and there. I just got beads very recently, and once in a while I feel comfortable chanting, and once in a while not comfortable at all. Maybe I don't chant properly. I don't know.

Śrīla Prabhupāda: Yes, everything has a process. You have to adopt the process.

Bob: The devotees tell me of the ecstasy they feel when chanting.

Śrīla Prabhupāda: Yes, the more you become purified, the more you will feel ecstasy. This chanting is the purifying process.

SIX

The Perfect Devotee

Māyāpur, India—February 29, 1972, evening

Bob: Śrīla Prabhupāda, earlier today we were discussing the need to practise austerity in Kṛṣṇa consciousness. Can you say something more about that?

Śrīla Prabhupāda: Yes, under the direction of the spiritual master one should practise austerities. You have no mind to follow austerities, but when you accept a spiritual master you have to carry out his order. That is austerity.

Śyāmasundara: Even if you don't want to practise austerity, you must.

Śrīla Prabhupāda: Yes, you must. Because you have surrendered to your spiritual master, his order is final. So even if you don't like it, you have to do it. To please me.

Śyāmasundara: Ah.

Śrīla Prabhupāda: But you don't like it. [*He laughs.*] Nobody likes to fast, but the spiritual master says, 'Today, fasting,' so what can be done? [*Śyāmasundara laughs.*] A disciple is one who has voluntarily agreed to be disciplined by the spiritual master. That is austerity.

Śyāmasundara: Many people in the material world may be completely enamoured by material life, and they don't want to undergo any austerity or bodily pain, but still they must. They are forced by nature to suffer austerities.

Śrīla Prabhupāda: That is forced austerity. That is not good. Only voluntary austerity will help.

Śyāmasundara: But if you don't undergo voluntary austerity, then you must be forced to undergo austerity?

Śrīla Prabhupāda: That is the difference between man and animal. An animal cannot accept austerity voluntarily, but a man can accept it. Suppose there are some nice sweetmeats in the confectioner's shop. A man wants to eat them, but he sees that he has no money so he restrains himself. But when a cow comes, immediately she pushes her mouth in. You may beat her with a stick, but she will tolerate it. Therefore an animal cannot undergo austerity.

But our austerity is very nice. We chant Hare Kṛṣṇa and dance, and then Kṛṣṇa sends very nice food and we eat. That's all. Why are you not agreeable to such austerity? Chanting, dancing, and eating nicely? And because we are following austerities, Kṛṣṇa sends us nice things. So we are not losers. When you become Kṛṣṇa-ized, you get *more* comforts than at the present moment. That's a fact. I have been living alone for the last twenty years, but I have no difficulties. Before taking *sannyāsa* I was living in Delhi. And although I was living alone, I had no difficulties.

Śyāmasundara: If you don't accept spiritual discipline, then nature will force so many calamities.

Śrīla Prabhupāda: Oh, yes. Kṛṣṇa states that in the *Bhagavad-gītā* [7.14]:

daivī hy eṣā guṇa-mayī
mama māyā duratyayā
mām eva ye prapadyante
māyām etāṁ taranti te

['This divine energy of Mine, consisting of the three modes of material nature, is difficult to overcome. But those who have surrendered unto Me can easily cross beyond it.'] *Māyā* is imposing so many difficulties, but as soon as you surrender to Kṛṣṇa, no more imposition.

Śyāmasundara: We were so foolish that we were always thinking, 'In the future I'll be happy.'

Śrīla Prabhupāda: Yes, that is *māyā,* illusion. That is like the ass. You sit down on the back of the ass and hold a morsel of food in front of its face. The ass is thinking, 'Let me go forward a little, and I shall get the grass.' [*Bob laughs.*] But it is always one foot distant. That is ass-ism. [*They all laugh.*] Everyone is thinking, 'Let me go a little forward, and I'll get it. I'll be very happy.'

[*There is a long pause, filled with the sound of bicycle horns, children playing, and throngs of people calling to one another.*]

Bob: I thank you so much. Tomorrow I'll have to leave you.

Śrīla Prabhupāda: Don't talk *l-e-a-v-e,* but talk *l-i-v-e.*

Bob: I cannot yet. I must return to my town tomorrow.

Śrīla Prabhupāda: Don't return.

Bob: I should stay here tomorrow?

Śrīla Prabhupāda: Stay here.

Bob: If you tell me to, I'll stay.

Śrīla Prabhupāda: Yes, you are a very good boy. [*There is a long pause. It is now much quieter.*] It is very simple. When the living entities forget Kṛṣṇa, they are in this material world. 'Kṛṣṇa' means His name, His form, His abode, His pastimes—everything. When we speak of a king, it means the king's government, his palace, his queen, his sons, his secretaries, his military strength, his activities—everything. Is it not?

Bob: Yes.

Śrīla Prabhupāda: Similarly, since Kṛṣṇa is the Supreme Personality of Godhead, as soon as we think of Kṛṣṇa, this means we are in touch with Kṛṣṇa and all His energies. That is complete by saying 'Rādhā-Kṛṣṇa.' Rādhā represents all the energies of Kṛṣṇa, and Kṛṣṇa is the Supreme Lord. So when we speak of Kṛṣṇa, the living entities are also included because the living entities are one of the energies of Kṛṣṇa—His superior energy. When this energy is not serving the energetic, that is material existence. The whole world is not serving Kṛṣṇa. Or, they are serving Kṛṣṇa indirectly, just as disobedient citizens serve the government indirectly. Prisoners come to the prison house on account of their disobedience of the laws of the state. But in the prison house they are forced to obey the laws of the state. Similarly, all the living entities here are godless, either by ignorance or by choice. They do not like to accept the supremacy of God. Demoniac. So we are trying to bring them to their original condition. That is the Kṛṣṇa consciousness movement.

Bob: I'd like to ask you about something I talked with the devotees about: medicine. I walked to the river with some devotees today. I have a cold, so I said I shouldn't go in the water. Some felt I should because it is the Ganges, and some said I shouldn't because I have a cold, and we were talking, and I don't understand. Do we get sick because of our bad actions in the past?

Śrīla Prabhupāda: Yes, that's a fact. Any kind of distress we suffer is due to our impious activities in the past.

Bob: But when someone is removed from karmic influence, does he still get sick?

Śrīla Prabhupāda: No. Or, even if he gets sick, that is very temporary. For instance, this fan is moving. If you disconnect the electric power, the fan will move for a few moments. That movement is not due to the electric current. It is due to—what is it called?

Śyāmasundara: Momentum.

Śrīla Prabhupāda: Momentum. But as soon as the momentum is gone, no more movement. Similarly, even if a devotee who has surrendered to Kṛṣṇa is suffering from material consequences, that is temporary. Therefore, a devotee does not take any material miseries as miseries. He takes them as Kṛṣṇa's, God's, mercy.

Bob: That attitude seems possible only for a perfected soul.

Śrīla Prabhupāda: A perfected soul is one who engages twenty-four hours a day in Kṛṣṇa consciousness. That is perfection. That is a transcendental position. Perfection means to engage in one's original consciousness. That Kṛṣṇa states in the *Bhagavad-gītā* [8.15]:

mām upetya punar janma
duḥkhālayam aśāśvatam
nāpnuvanti mahātmānaḥ
saṁsiddhiṁ paramāṁ gatāḥ

'Anyone who comes to Me does not return to this miserable, temporary material world. That is complete perfection.' *Saṁsiddhi. Siddhi* is perfection. That is Brahman realization, spiritual realization. And *saṁsiddhi* means devotion, which comes after Brahman realization.

Bob: Could you just say that last thing again please?

Śrīla Prabhupāda: *Saṁsiddhi.*

Bob: Yes.

Śrīla Prabhupāda: *Sam* means 'complete,' and *siddhi* means 'perfection.' In the *Bhagavad-gītā* it is stated that one who goes back home, back to Godhead, has attained complete perfection. So perfection comes when one realizes that he is not this body; he is spirit soul. That is the *brahma-bhūta* stage, called Brahman realization. That is perfection. And *saṁsiddhi,* complete perfection, comes after Brahman realization, when one engages in devotional service. Therefore if one is already engaged in devotional service, it is to be understood that Brahman realization is there. Therefore it is called *saṁsiddhi.*

Bob: I ask you this very humbly, but do you feel diseases and sickness?

Śrīla Prabhupāda: Yes.

Bob: Is this a result of your past *karma*?

Śrīla Prabhupāda: Yes.

Bob: So one in this material world never escapes his *karma* completely?

Śrīla Prabhupāda: Yes, he escapes. No more *karma* for a devotee. No more karmic reaction.
Bob: But you must be the best devotee.
Śrīla Prabhupāda: No, I don't consider myself the best devotee. I am the lowest.
Bob: No!
Śrīla Prabhupāda: *You* are the best devotee.
Bob: [*Laughs.*] Oh, no, no! What you say always seems right, so you must be the best devotee.
Śrīla Prabhupāda: The thing is that even the best devotee comes to the second-class platform when he preaches.
Bob: What would the best devotee be doing?
Śrīla Prabhupāda: The best devotee does not preach.
Bob: What does he do?
Śrīla Prabhupāda: He sees that there is no need of preaching. For him, everyone is a devotee. [*Bob laughs heartily.*] Yes, he sees no more nondevotees—all devotees. He is called an *uttama-adhikārī.* But while I am preaching, how can I say I am the best devotee? Just like Rādhārāṇī—She does not see anyone as a nondevotee. Therefore we try to approach Rādhārāṇī.
Bob: Who is this?
Śrīla Prabhupāda: Rādhārāṇī, Kṛṣṇa's consort.
Bob: Ah.
Śrīla Prabhupāda: If anyone approaches Rādhārāṇī, She recommends to Kṛṣṇa, 'Here is the best devotee; he is better than Me,' and Kṛṣṇa cannot refuse him. That is the best devotee. But it is not to be imitated: 'I have become the best devotee.' *Īśvare tad-adhīneṣu bāliśeṣu dviṣatsu ca.* A second-class devotee has the vision that some are envious of God, but this is not the vision of the best devotee. The best devotee sees, 'Nobody is envious of God. Everyone is better than me.' Just like *Caitanya-caritāmṛta's* author, Kṛṣṇadāsa Kavirāja. He says, 'I am lower than the worm in the stool.'
Bob: Who is saying this?

Śrīla Prabhupāda: Kṛṣṇadāsa Kavirāja, the author of *Caitanya-caritāmṛta: purīṣera kīṭa haite muñi se laghiṣṭha.* He is not making a show. He is feeling like that. 'I am the lowest. Everyone is best, but I am the lowest. Everyone else is engaged in Kṛṣṇa's service, but I am not engaged.' Caitanya Mahāprabhu said, 'Oh, I have not a pinch of devotion to Kṛṣṇa. I cry to make a show. If I had been a devotee of Kṛṣṇa, I would have died long ago. But I am living. That is the proof that I do not love Kṛṣṇa.' That is the vision of the best devotee. He is so much absorbed in Kṛṣṇa's love that he says, 'Everyone else is a devotee, but I am the lowest. Therefore I cannot see God.' That is the best devotee.

Bob: So a devotee must work for everybody's liberation?

Śrīla Prabhupāda: Yes. A devotee must work under the direction of a bona fide spiritual master, not imitate the best devotee.

Śyāmasundara: Once you said that sometimes you feel sickness or pain due to the sinful activities of your devotees. Can disease sometimes be due to that?

Śrīla Prabhupāda: You see, Kṛṣṇa says, *ahaṁ tvāṁ sarva-pāpebhyo mokṣayiṣyāmi mā śucaḥ:* 'I will deliver you from all sinful reaction. Do not fear.' Kṛṣṇa is so powerful that He can take up all the sins of others and immediately make them right. But when a living entity acts on behalf of Kṛṣṇa, he also takes the responsibility for the sinful activities of his devotees. Therefore to become a *guru* is not an easy task. You see? He has to take all the poisons and absorb them. So sometimes—because he is not Kṛṣṇa—there is some trouble.

Therefore Caitanya Mahāprabhu has forbidden, 'Don't make many disciples.' But for preaching work, to expand the preaching, we have to accept many disciples, even if we suffer. That's a fact. The spiritual master has to take the responsibility for all the sinful activities of his disciples. Therefore to make many disciples is a risky job unless one is able to assimilate all the sins.

vāñchā-kalpa-tarubhyaś ca
kṛpā-sindhubhya eva ca

patitānāṁ pāvanebhyo
vaiṣṇavebhyo namo namaḥ

['I offer my respectful obeisances unto all the Vaiṣṇava devotees of the Lord. Just like desire trees, they can fulfill the desires of everyone, and they are full of compassion for the fallen conditioned souls.'] The spiritual master takes responsibility for all the fallen souls. That idea is also in the Bible. Jesus Christ took all the sinful reactions of the people and sacrificed his life. That is the responsibility of a spiritual master. Because Kṛṣṇa is Kṛṣṇa, He is *apāpa-viddha*—He cannot be attacked by sinful reactions. But a living entity is sometimes subjected to their influence because he is so small. Big fire, small fire. If you put some big thing in a small fire, the fire itself may be extinguished. But in a big fire, whatever you put in is burned up. The big fire can consume anything.

Bob: Christ's suffering was of that nature?

Śrīla Prabhupāda: He took the sinful reactions of all the people. Therefore he suffered.

Bob: I see.

Śrīla Prabhupāda: In the Bible it is said that he took all the sinful reactions of the people and sacrificed his life. But these Christian people have made it a law for Christ to suffer while they do all nonsense. Such great fools they are! They have let Jesus Christ make a contract for taking all their sinful reactions so they can go on with all nonsense. That is their religion. Christ was so magnanimous that he took all their sins and suffered, but that does not induce them to *stop* all these sins. They have not come to that sense. They have taken it very easily: 'Let Lord Jesus Christ suffer, and we'll do all nonsense.' Is it not?

Bob: It is so.

Śrīla Prabhupāda: They should have been ashamed: 'Lord Jesus Christ suffered for us, but we are continuing the sinful activities.' He told everyone, 'Thou shalt not kill,' but they are indulging in killing, thinking, 'Lord Jesus Christ will excuse us and take all the sinful reactions.' This is going on.

We should be very cautious: 'For my sinful actions my spiritual master will suffer, so I'll not commit even a pinch of sinful activities.' That is the duty of the disciple. After initiation, all sinful reaction is finished. Now if he again commits sinful activities, his spiritual master has to suffer. A disciple should be sympathetic and consider that for his sinful activities his spiritual master will suffer. If the spiritual master is attacked by some disease, it is due to the sinful activities of others. Therefore the injunction is 'Don't make many disciples.' But we do it because we are preaching. Never mind, let us suffer; still we shall accept these disciples.

So your question was whether when I suffer it is due to my past misdeeds. Was it not? *That* is my misdeed—that I accepted some disciples who are nonsense. That is my misdeed.

Bob: This happens on occasion?

Śrīla Prabhupāda: Yes. This is sure to happen because we are accepting so many disciples. It is the duty of the disciples to be cautious. 'My spiritual master has saved me. I should not put him again into suffering.' Of course, when the spiritual master is suffering, Kṛṣṇa saves him. Kṛṣṇa thinks, 'Oh, he has taken so much responsibility for delivering fallen persons.' So Kṛṣṇa says, *kaunteya pratijānīhi na me bhaktaḥ praṇaśyati:* 'O son of Kuntī, declare it boldly that My devotee never perishes.' The spiritual master is protected because he takes the risk on account of Kṛṣṇa.

Bob: Your suffering is not the same kind of pain we feel.

Śrīla Prabhupāda: No, it is not due to *karma.* The pain is there sometimes, so that the disciples may know, 'Due to our sinful activities, our spiritual master is suffering.'

Bob: You look very well now.

Śrīla Prabhupāda: I am always well in the sense that even if there is suffering I know Kṛṣṇa will protect me. But this suffering is not due to *my* sinful activities.

Bob: In the town I live in, I take boiled water because some of the water has disease in it. Now, why should I drink boiled water if I have been good enough not to get a disease? Then I may drink any water. And if I have been not acting properly, then I shall get disease anyway.

Śrīla Prabhupāda: So long as you are in the material world, you cannot neglect physical laws. Suppose you go to a jungle and there is a tiger. It is known that it will attack you, so why should you voluntarily go and be attacked? It is not that a devotee should take unnecessary physical risks. He shouldn't think, 'Now that I have become a devotee, I challenge everything.' That is foolishness.

anāsaktasya viṣayān
yathārham upayuñjataḥ
nirbandhaḥ kṛṣṇa-sambandhe
yuktaṁ vairāgyam ucyate

The devotee is advised to accept the necessities of life without attachment. He'll take boiled water, but if boiled water is not available, does it mean he will not drink water? If it is not available, he will drink ordinary water. We take Kṛṣṇa *prasādam,* but while touring we sometimes have to take some food in a hotel. Because one is a devotee, should he think, 'I will not take any food from the hotel. I shall starve'? If I starve, then I will be weak and will not be able to preach.

Bob: Does a devotee lose some of his individuality?

Śrīla Prabhupāda: No, he has full individuality for pleasing Kṛṣṇa. Kṛṣṇa says, 'You surrender unto Me.' So he voluntarily surrenders. It is not that he has lost his individuality. He keeps his individuality. Just like Arjuna: in the beginning he was declining to fight on account of his individuality. But when he accepted Kṛṣṇa as his spiritual master, he became a disciple. Then whatever Kṛṣṇa ordered, he said yes. That doesn't mean he lost his individuality. He voluntarily accepted: 'Whatever Kṛṣṇa says, I shall do it.'

Or just like all my disciples: they have not lost their individuality, but they have surrendered their individuality. That is required. For example, suppose a man does not indulge in sex. It does not mean he has become impotent. If he likes, he can have sex a thousand times. But he has voluntarily avoided it. *Paraṁ dṛṣṭvā nivartate:* he has a higher taste. Sometimes we fast, but that does not mean we are diseased. We voluntarily fast. It does not mean that I am not hungry or cannot eat. But we voluntarily fast.

Bob: Does the devotee who surrenders keep his individual taste for different things?

Śrīla Prabhupāda: Yes.

Bob: Does he keep his individual likes and dislikes?

Śrīla Prabhupāda: Yes, he keeps everything in full. But he gives preference to Kṛṣṇa. Suppose I like something but Kṛṣṇa says, 'No, you cannot use it.' Then I shall not use it. I give it up for Kṛṣṇa's sake. Positively, Kṛṣṇa says, 'I like these things.' So we have to offer to Kṛṣṇa what He likes, and then we take *prasādam*. Kṛṣṇa likes Rādhārāṇī. Therefore all the *gopīs* are trying to push Rādharāṇī to Kṛṣṇa. 'Kṛṣṇa likes this *gopī*. All right, push Her forward to Him.' That is Kṛṣṇa consciousness—to satisfy the senses of Kṛṣṇa, not to satisfy my senses. That is *bhakti*. That is called *prema,* love for Kṛṣṇa. 'Ah, Kṛṣṇa likes this. I must give Him this.'

Bob: Some *prasādam* I like, and some I find not at all to my liking.

Śrīla Prabhupāda: You should not do that. The perfection is that whatever is offered to Kṛṣṇa you should accept. That is perfection. You cannot say, 'I like this, I don't like this.' So long as you make such discrimination, that means you have not appreciated what *prasādam* is. No disliking, no liking. Whatever Kṛṣṇa likes, that's all right.

A devotee: But suppose someone prepares something for Kṛṣṇa but does not make it so nicely.

Śrīla Prabhupāda: No, if made sincerely with devotion, then Kṛṣṇa will like it. Just like Vidura. Vidura was feeding Kṛṣṇa bananas, but he was so absorbed in thought that he was throwing away the real bananas and giving Kṛṣṇa the skin, and Kṛṣṇa was eating. [*All laugh.*] Kṛṣṇa knew that he was giving Him the skins in devotion, and Kṛṣṇa can eat anything, provided there is devotion. It doesn't matter whether it is materially tasty or not. Similarly, a devotee also takes Kṛṣṇa *prasādam* whether it is tasty or not. We should accept everything.

A devotee: But if the devotion is not there?

Śrīla Prabhupāda: If devotion is not there, Kṛṣṇa doesn't like any food, either tasty or not tasty. He does not accept it.

A devotee: In India…

Śrīla Prabhupāda: Oh, India, India. Don't talk of India! Talk of philosophy. If there is no devotion, Kṛṣṇa does not accept anything, whether in India or in your country. Lord Kṛṣṇa is not obliged to accept anything costly because it is very tasty. Kṛṣṇa has very many tasty dishes in Vaikuṇṭha. He is not hankering after your food. He accepts your devotion, *bhakti.* The real thing is devotion, not the food. Kṛṣṇa does not accept any food of this material world. He accepts only the devotion.

patraṁ puṣpaṁ phalaṁ toyaṁ
yo me bhaktyā prayacchati
tad ahaṁ bhakty-upahṛtam
aśnāmi prayatātmanaḥ

'If one offers Me with love and devotion a leaf, a flower, a fruit or water, I will accept it, because it has been offered to Me with devotion and love' [Bg. 9.26] It is devotion that is required. Therefore we do not allow anyone to cook who is not a devotee. Kṛṣṇa does not accept anything from the hands of a nondevotee. Why should He accept? He is not hungry. He does not require any food. He accepts only the devotion, that's all. That is the main point.

So one has to become a devotee, not a good cook. But if he is a devotee, then he will be a good cook also. Automatically he will become a good cook. Therefore one has to become a devotee only. Then all other good qualifications will automatically be there. And if he is a nondevotee, any good qualifications have no value. He is on the mental plane, so he has no good qualification.

Bob: I still do not understand so much about *prasādam.*

Śrīla Prabhupāda: *Prasādam* is always *prasādam.* But because we are not elevated sufficiently, therefore we do not like some *prasādam.*

Bob: I find that some *prasādam* is too spicy and hurts my stomach.

Śrīla Prabhupāda: Well, that is also due to not appreciating, but the cook should have some consideration. Kṛṣṇa must be offered first-class foods. So if the cook offers something last class, he is not performing his duty. But Kṛṣṇa can accept anything if it is offered by a devotee, and a devotee can accept any *prasādam,* even if it is spicy. Hiraṇyakaśipu gave his son poison, and after offering it to Kṛṣṇa the son drank it as nectar and remained unharmed.

So even if *prasādam* is very spicy to others, it is very palatable to the devotee. What is the question of spicy? Kṛṣṇa was offered poison, real poison, by Putanā Rākṣasī. But He is so nice that He thought, 'She came to Me as My mother.' So He took the poison and delivered her. Kṛṣṇa does not take the bad side. A good man does not take the bad side—he takes only the good side. Just like one of my Godbrothers: he wanted to make business with my Guru Mahārāja [spiritual master]. But my Guru Mahārāja did not take the bad side. He took the good side. He thought, 'He has come forward to give me some service.'

Bob: Let us say some devotee has some medical trouble and cannot eat a certain type of food. For instance, some devotees do not eat ghee because of liver trouble. So should these devotees also take all kinds of *prasādam*?

Śrīla Prabhupāda: No, no. Those who are not perfect devotees may discriminate. But a perfect devotee does not discriminate. Why should you imitate a perfect devotee? So long as you have discrimination, you are not a perfect devotee. So why should you artificially imitate a perfect devotee and eat everything?

The point is, a perfect devotee does not make any discrimination. Whatever is offered to Kṛṣṇa is nectar. That's all. Kṛṣṇa accepts anything from a devotee. 'Whatever is offered to Me by My devotee, I accept.' The same thing is true for a pure devotee. Don't you see the point? A perfect devotee does not make any discrimination. But if I am not a perfect devotee and I discriminate, why should I imitate the perfect devotee? It may not be possible for me to digest everything because I am not a perfect devotee. A devotee should not be a foolish man. It is said: *kṛṣṇa ye bhaje se baḍa catura*. So a devotee knows his position, and he is intelligent enough to deal with others accordingly.

SEVEN

Acting in Knowledge of Kṛṣṇa

Māyāpur, India—February 29, 1972 (evening, continued)

An Indian gentleman: By what kind of actions does one earn good *karma*?

Śrīla Prabhupāda: Good *karma* means what is prescribed in the *Vedas.* Specifically, it is prescribed that one should perform *yajña. Yajña* means actions for the satisfaction of Lord Viṣṇu, the Supreme Personality of Godhead. So good *karma* means performance of the *yajñas* as they are prescribed in the Vedic literatures.

A good, law-abiding citizen is one whose actions satisfy the government. So, good *karma* is actions that satisfy Lord Viṣṇu, the Supreme Lord. Unfortunately, modern people do not know what the Supreme Personality of Godhead is, what to speak of satisfying Him. They are simply busy with material activities. Therefore all of them are performing only bad *karma* and therefore suffering. They are blind men leading other blind men. And all are then suffering by bad *karma.* That is very easy to understand. If you do something criminal, you will suffer. If you do something benevolent for the state, for the people, then you are recognized; you are sometimes given a title. This is good and bad *karma.*

So, by good *karma* you enjoy some material happiness, and by bad *karma* you suffer from material distress. By good *karma* you get birth in a good family; you get riches, good money. Then you become a learned scholar; you become beautiful also.

Bob: What about the person who is not very aware of God, but…

Śrīla Prabhupāda: Then he is an animal. A person who does not know what is God, or one who does not try to understand what is God—he is an animal.

Bob: What about innocent people?

Śrīla Prabhupāda: The animal is very innocent. If you cut its throat, it won't protest. So innocence is not a very good qualification. Our proposition is that one must be very, very intelligent, and then he can understand Kṛṣṇa. To become an innocent, ignorant simpleton is not a very good qualification. Simplicity is all right, but one should not be unintelligent.

Bob: Can you tell me what intelligence is?

Śrīla Prabhupāda: Intelligence means to know what one is, what this world is, what God is, and what their interrelations are. The animal does not know what he is. He thinks that he is the body. Similarly, anyone who does not know what he is is not intelligent.

Bob: What about a person who tries to do what is right and is very conscientious about the things he does? Like the servant who is very honest to his master but knows that if he were not honest he would not be caught. If a person like that stays honest anyway, is that some kind of good *karma*?

Śrīla Prabhupāda: Yes, to become honest is also good *karma.* How to become a good man is described in the *Bhagavad-gītā* very elaborately: *daivī sampad vimokṣāya nibandhāyāsurī matā.* So, if you become qualified with *daivī sampad,* transcendental qualities, then *vimokṣāya,* you will be liberated. And *nibandhāyāsurī*—if you have demoniac qualities you will be more and more entangled. Unfortunately, modern people do not know what is liberation and what is entanglement. They are so ignorant; they do not know.

If I ask you what liberation is, can you answer? [*No answer.*] And if I ask you what entanglement is, can you answer? [*Again no answer.*] These words are there in the Vedic literature—liberation and entanglement—but, at the present moment people do not even know what they mean. They are so ignorant and foolish, and still they are proud of their advancement in knowledge. You are a professor, a teacher; can you explain what liberation is?

Bob: Not adequately, because if I could explain it then I would become liberated very fast.

Śrīla Prabhupāda: But if you do not know what liberation is, then where is the question of fast or slow liberation? You should first know what liberation is. If you do not know where the train is going, then what is the use of knowing whether it is going fast or slow? So, what is liberation? You daily ask *me.* Now I am asking *you.*

Bob: [*Laughs.*] Ah—okay... Let me think for a moment.

Śrīla Prabhupāda: Liberation is described in the *Śrīmad-Bhāgavatam.* The exact Sanskrit word for liberation is *mukti.* So that is defined in the *Śrīmad-Bhāgavatam: muktir hitvānyathā rūpaṁ svarūpena vyavasthitiḥ.* One should stop doing all nonsense and become situated in his original position. That is liberation. Unfortunately, today nobody knows his original position or how to act properly in that position. The modern population is so ignorant about their life—it is a very awkward position. They do not know.

Bob: Can you tell me who is honest?

Śrīla Prabhupāda: If one does not know what is honesty, how can he be honest? But if you know what is honesty, then you can be honest. What is honesty? First of all explain.

Bob: I would say that honesty is doing what you really feel is right.

Śrīla Prabhupāda: A thief is feeling, 'I must steal to provide for my children. It is right.' Does it mean that he is honest? The butcher thinks, 'I must cut the throat of the animals daily. It is my livelihood.' Nārada Muni once met a hunter and asked him, 'Why are you killing in this way?' And he said, 'Oh, it is my business. My father taught it to me.' The hunter was honestly doing his work.

So, a feeling of honesty depends on culture. A thief's culture is different from ours. He thinks stealing is honest.

Bob: So, what is honesty?

Śrīla Prabhupāda: Yes, that is my question. [*Everyone laughs.*] Real honesty is that you should not encroach upon another's property. This is honesty. For instance, this is my table. If you want to take it away, is that honesty? Therefore, the simple definition of honesty is that you should not encroach upon another's rights. That is honesty.

Bob: So somebody who is honest would be in the mode of goodness? Would that be correct?

Śrīla Prabhupāda: Certainly, certainly. Because the mode of goodness means knowledge. So if you know, 'This table does not belong to me; it belongs to Swamiji,' you will not try to take it away. Therefore, one must know to whom things belong; then he can be honest.

Bob: You have said that the mode of goodness was knowledge of God, but somebody may be honest without having very much knowledge of God. Without thinking they are honest because it is God's wish, they just feel like they ought to be honest.

Śrīla Prabhupāda: God wishes everyone to be honest. Why should God think otherwise?

Bob: Can you follow God's wishes without knowing you are following God's wishes?

Śrīla Prabhupāda: No, following without knowing—that is absurd. You must know the order of God. And if you follow that, then that is honesty.

Bob: So somebody cannot really be honest without knowing God?

Śrīla Prabhupāda: Yes, because God is the supreme proprietor, the supreme enjoyer, and the supreme friend. That is the statement of the *Bhagavad-gītā.* If anyone knows these three things, then he is in full knowledge. These three things only: that God is the proprietor of everything, God is friend of everyone, and God is the enjoyer of everything. For example, everyone knows that in the body the stomach is the enjoyer—not the hands, legs, eyes, ears. These are there simply to help the stomach. For example, the eyes—the vulture goes seven miles up to see where there is food. Then the wings fly there, and the jaws catch the food. But the ultimate enjoyer of the food is the stomach. Is it not?

Bob: That is so.

Śrila Prabhupāda: Similarly, as in this body the stomach is the enjoyer, the central figure of the whole cosmic manifestation, material or spiritual, is Kṛṣṇa, God. He is the enjoyer. We can understand this just by considering our own bodies. The body is also a creation. The body has the same mechanical nature you will find in the whole universe. The same mechanical arrangement will be found anywhere you go, even in animals. In the human body or in the cosmic manifestation—almost the same mechanism. So you can understand very easily that in this body—any body, your body—the stomach is the enjoyer. There is a central enjoyer. And the stomach is the friend also. Because if you cannot digest food, you see, then all other limbs of the body become weak. Therefore the stomach is the friend. It is digesting and distributing the energy to all the limbs of the body. Is it not?

Bob: It is so.

Śrila Prabhupāda: Similarly, the central 'stomach' of the whole creation is God, or Kṛṣṇa. He is the enjoyer, He is the friend, and, as the supreme proprietor, He is maintaining everyone, just as a king can maintain the whole country's citizens because he is the proprietor. Without being the proprietor, how can one become everyone's friend?

So these things have to be understood. Kṛṣṇa is the supreme enjoyer, Kṛṣṇa is the supreme proprietor, and Kṛṣṇa is the supreme friend. If you know these three things, then your knowledge is full; you do not require to understand anything more. *Yasmin vijñāte sarvam evaṁ vijñātaṁ bhavati.* If you simply understand Kṛṣṇa by this formula, then your knowledge is complete. You don't require any more knowledge. But people will not agree.

'Why should Kṛṣṇa be the proprietor? Hitler should be the proprietor. Nixon…' That is going on. Therefore you are in trouble. But if you understand these three things only, then your knowledge is complete. But we will not accept. We will put forward so many impediments to understanding these three things, and that is the cause of our trouble. But in the *Bhagavad-gītā* [5.29] Kṛṣṇa plainly says:

bhoktāraṁ yajña-tapasāṁ
sarva-loka-maheśvaram
suhṛdaṁ sarva-bhūtānāṁ
jñātvā māṁ śāntim ṛcchati

['A person in full consciousness of Me, knowing Me to be the ultimate beneficiary of all sacrifices and austerities, the Supreme Lord of all planets and demigods, and the benefactor and well-wisher of all living entities, attains peace from the pangs of material miseries.'] But we won't take this. We put forward so many false proprietors, false friends, false enjoyers, and they fight one another. This is the situation of the world. If people would take this knowledge, there would immediately be peace (*śāntim ṛcchati*). This is knowledge, and if anyone follows this principle, he is honest. He does not claim, 'It is mine.' He knows, 'Everything is Kṛṣṇa's, so therefore everything should be utilized for Kṛṣṇa's service.' That is honesty. If this pencil belongs to me, the etiquette is for my students to ask, 'Can I use this pencil?' Then I will reply, 'Yes, you can.'

Similarly, if I know that everything belongs to Kṛṣṇa, I will not use anything without His permission. That is honesty. And that is knowledge. One who does not know this is ignorant; he is foolish. And a foolish man commits crimes. All criminals are foolish men. Out of ignorance one breaks the law. So ignorance is not bliss, but it is folly to be wise where ignorance is bliss. That is the difficulty. The whole world is enjoying ignorance. And when you talk about

Kṛṣṇa consciousness, they do not very much appreciate it. If I say, 'Kṛṣṇa is the proprietor; you are not the proprietor,' you will not be very much satisfied. [*Everyone laughs.*] Just see—ignorance is bliss.

So it is my foolishness to say the real truth. Therefore it is folly to be wise where ignorance is bliss. So we are taking the risk of offending people, and they think we are fools. If I say to a rich man, 'You are not the proprietor; Kṛṣṇa is the proprietor. So whatever money you have, spend it for Kṛṣṇa,' he will be angry. *Upadeśo hi mūrkhānāṁ prakopāya na śāntaye:* 'If you instruct a rascal, he'll become angry.' Therefore we go as beggars: 'My dear sir, you are a very nice man. I am a *sannyāsī* beggar, so I want to construct a temple. Can you spare some money?' So he will think, 'Oh, here is a beggar. Give him some money.' [*Everyone laughs.*] But if I say, 'Dear sir, you have millions of dollars at your disposal. That is Kṛṣṇa's money. Give it to me. I am Kṛṣṇa's servant'—oh, he'll chase me away. [*Everyone laughs.*] He will not be very satisfied. Rather, if I go as a beggar, he will give me something. And if I tell him the truth, he will not give me a farthing. [*Everyone laughs.*] We convince him as beggars. We are not beggars; we are Kṛṣṇa's servants.

For ourselves we don't want anything from anyone, because we know Kṛṣṇa will provide everything. This is knowledge. For instance, a child will sometimes take a hundred dollar bill, so we have to flatter him. 'Oh, you are so nice. Please take these lozenges and give me that paper. It is nothing; it is paper.' And he will say, 'Oh, yes. Take. That's nice.' And he returns the hundred-dollar note for two-penny sweets. So we have to beg people in that way. Why? Because a man will go to hell by taking Kṛṣṇa's money. So some way or other, take some money from him and engage him in the Kṛṣṇa consciousness movement.

Bob: And then he may not go to hell?

Śrīla Prabhupāda: Yes. You save him from going to hell. Because a farthing spent for Krsna will be noted by Him: 'Oh, this man has given a farthing.' This is called *ajñāta-sukṛti* [devotional service performed unknowingly]. People are generally very poor in their thought; therefore the saintly persons move among them just to enlighten them a little, to give them a chance to serve Kṛṣṇa. That is the saintly person's duty. But if someone takes money from others and utilizes it for his sense gratification, then he goes to hell. Then he is finished. He is a cheater, a criminal. You cannot take a farthing from anyone and use it for your own sense gratification.

Bob: I think of people I know who are not Kṛṣṇa conscious.

Śrīla Prabhupāda: Kṛṣṇa means God.

Bob: They are just slightly God conscious, but still these people are honest to the extent that they don't take from other people at all. And they try to be honest with other people.

Śrīla Prabhupāda: They do not take from other people, but they take from God.

Bob: So these people are half-good?

Śrīla Prabhupāda: Not good. If they do not learn this principle—that God is the proprietor—they cannot be good.

Bob: I'm thinking of poor people who need money and food but do not commit crimes to get it. Everybody around them may be stealing, but they still stand up and don't steal. These people somehow deserve something good to happen to them.

Śrīla Prabhupāda: But the man who is thinking he is not stealing is also a thief because he does not know that everything belongs to Kṛṣṇa. Therefore, whatever he is accepting, he is stealing.

Bob: Is he less of a thief?

Śrīla Prabhupāda: You may not know that I am the proprietor of this shawl, but if you take it away, are you not stealing?

Bob: But maybe if I know it is yours and I take it I am a worse thief than if I do not know whose it is. I just think it may be nobody's, and I take it.

Śrīla Prabhupāda: That is also stealing, because it must belong to somebody. And you are taking it without his permission. You may not know exactly who the proprietor is, but you know it must belong to someone. Sometimes we see on the road so many valuable things left there—government property for repairing roads or some electrical work. A man may think, 'Oh, fortunately these things are lying here, so I may take them.' Is it not stealing?

Bob: It is stealing.

Śrīla Prabhupāda: Yes. He does not know that it is all government property and he takes it away. That is stealing. And when he is caught, he is arrested, and he is punished. So, similarly, whatever you are collecting... Suppose you are drinking a glass of water from the river. Is the river your property?

Bob: No.

Śrīla Prabhupāda: Then? It is stealing. You have not created the river. You do not know who is the proprietor, but it is not your property. So, even if you drink a glass of water without knowing to whom it belongs, you are a thief. So you may think, 'I am honest,' but actually you are a thief. You must remember Kṛṣṇa. 'Oh, Kṛṣṇa, it is Your creation, so kindly allow me to drink.' This is honesty. Therefore a devotee always thinks of Kṛṣṇa. In all activities: 'Oh, it is Kṛṣṇa's.' This is honesty. So without Kṛṣṇa consciousness, everyone is a rascal, a thief, a rogue, a robber.

Therefore our conclusion is that anyone who does not understand Kṛṣṇa has no good qualifications. He is not honest, nor has he knowledge. Therefore he is a third-class man. This is not dogmatism. This is a fact. So, you have understood what is knowledge and what is honesty?

Bob: In a way.

Śrīla Prabhupāda: And is there another way? [*Bob laughs.*] Is there any other way? Defy it! [*Bob laughs again. Śrīla Prabhupāda also laughs.*] Is there an alternative? We do not say anything that can be defied by anyone; that experience we have. Rather, we defy everyone: 'Any questions?' Till now, Kṛṣṇa has given us protection. In big, big meetings in big, big countries, after speaking I ask, 'Any questions?'

Bob: Now I have none.

Śrīla Prabhupāda: In London, we had lectures for twelve days in Conway Hall. So after every meeting I asked, 'Any questions?'

Bob: Did you get many questions?

Śrīla Prabhupāda: Oh, yes. But many were foolish questions.

Bob: Let me ask one more question. What is being foolish?

Śrīla Prabhupāda: One who has no knowledge is to be considered foolish.

An Indian gentleman: Prabhupāda, I have one question. Can I ask?

Śrīla Prabhupāda: Yes.

Indian gentleman: Some time ago in Calcutta they observed a week named 'Prevention of Cruelty to Animals Week.'

Śrīla Prabhupāda: Hmmm. This is another foolishness. They are advertising prevention of cruelty, yet they are maintaining thousands of slaughterhouses. You see? That is another foolishness. They are regularly cruel to animals, and they are making a society to prevent it. It is as if a gang of thieves calls itself Goodman and Company.

Girirāja: Yesterday you said that the spiritual master may have to suffer due to the sinful activities of his disciples. What do you mean by sinful activities?

Śrīla Prabhupāda: At initiation you promised, 'I shall follow the regulative principles.' If you do not follow, that is sinful. Very simple. You break the promise and do nasty things; therefore you are sinful. Is it not?

Girirāja: Yes. But there are some things we're instructed to do that, even though we try to do them, we cannot yet do perfectly.

Śrīla Prabhupāda: You try to do and cannot do? How is that?

Girirāja: Like chanting attentively. Sometimes we try to, but…

Śrīla Prabhupāda: Well, that is not a fault. Suppose you are trying to do something, but due to your inexperience you sometimes fail. That is not a fault. You are trying. A verse in the *Bhāgavatam* says that if a devotee is trying his best but due to his incapability he sometimes fails, Kṛṣṇa excuses him. And in the *Bhagavad-gītā* [9.30] Kṛṣṇa says, *api cet su-durācāro bhajate mām ananya-bhāk sādhur* *eva sa mantavyaḥ*. 'Someone may commit the most abominable activity, but if he is worshipping Me sincerely he should be considered a saintly person.' Sometimes one does something nonsensical unwillingly, due to past bad habits. That does not mean he is faulty. But he must repent for what he has done. And he should try to avoid it as far as possible. But habit is second nature. Sometimes, in spite of your trying hard, *māyā* is so strong that it trips you with pitfalls. That can be excused. Kṛṣṇa excuses. But those who are doing something willingly are not excused. On the strength that I am a devotee, if I think, 'Because I am chanting, I may therefore commit all this nonsense and it will be nullified,' that is the greatest offence.

EIGHT

Advancing in Kṛṣṇa Consciousness

(An exchange of letters)

Springfield, New Jersey
June 12, 1972

Dear Prabhupāda,

I offer my humble obeisances.

I have been associating with the devotees of the New York temple. With the association of such fine, advanced devotees, I hope that I may make some advancement in Kṛṣṇa consciousness. My fiancée has started to come to the temple and is chanting a little. She knew nothing about Kṛṣṇa consciousness until I wrote her about it from India. Ātreya Ṛṣi has been kind enough to invite us to his home so that we may see an ideal householder life.

I went to Bombay the end of April for termination from the Peace Corps. I was fortunate enough to come down with a minor illness, so that I had to stay in Bombay for two weeks. I spent the time with the advanced and kind devotees at Juhu. Unfortunately you had left five days previously.

I understand so little, but I have faith in the process of Kṛṣṇa consciousness and hope to take to it more and more.

I look forward to Ātreya Ṛṣi's description of the temple in Los Angeles and hope that I may personally hear you in New York.

Thank you for the kindness you have shown to a *very* undeserving boy.

Sincerely,
Bob Cohen

A. C. Bhaktivedanta Swami
ISKCON Los Angeles
June 16, 1972

Bob Cohen
Springfield, New Jersey

My dear Bob,

Please accept my blessings. I thank you very much for your letter dated June 12, 1972. I have noted the sentiments expressed therein with great pleasure. I am very glad to hear that you are associating with us. I know that you are a very good boy, very intelligent, and your behavior is gentle, so I have all confidence that very quickly Kṛṣṇa will bestow all His blessings upon you, and you will feel yourself becoming perfectly happy in Kṛṣṇa consciousness. One makes his advancement in Kṛṣṇa consciousness by voluntarily giving up his attachment to material nature, or *māyā*. Such renunciation is called *tapasya*. But we are not very willing to perform austerities without good reason; therefore any man with a good scientific and philosophical mind, like your good self, must first appreciate what transcendental knowledge is. If you get knowledge, automatically *tapasya* will follow, and then you make your advancement in spiritual life. So to get knowledge is the first item for anyone who is hoping to find the perfection of his life. Therefore I advise you to read our books daily as far as possible and try to understand the subject matter from different angles of vision by discussing it frequently with the devotees at the New York temple. In this way you will gradually become convinced, and by your sincere attitude and devotional service you will make progress.

Yes, having some faith in me and in this Kṛṣṇa consciousness process is the first and only requirement for getting actual wisdom. If there is faith, understanding will follow. And as your understanding increases, so will your disgust with the spell of illusory energy. And when you voluntarily give up your entanglements in the material world, then the progress is assured.

I think we are just now typing up the tapes of those conversations we held in Māyāpur, and we shall be publishing them as a book. It will be called *Perfect Questions, Perfect Answers.* I shall send you a copy as soon as they are ready to distribute. Meanwhile, I shall be stopping in New York for two or three days on my way to London for the Ratha-yātrā Festival there. I am not yet certain when I shall be arriving in New York, but it will be some time in the early part of July. You may keep in regular contact with Bali Mardana regarding the arrival date, and I shall be very much engladdened to meet with you in New York once again. Again we shall discuss if you have any questions.

Hoping this will meet you in good health and a happy mood,

Your ever well-wisher,
A.C. Bhaktivedanta Swami

NINE

Deciding for the Future

New York—July 4, 1972

Bob: I received your very kind letter about a week ago.

Śrīla Prabhupāda: You are a very intelligent boy. Try to understand this philosophy. It is very important. People are wasting so much energy for sense gratification. They are not aware of what is going to happen in the next life. There is a next life, but foolish people are ignorant. This life is a preparation for the next life. That they do not know. The modern education and its universities are completely in darkness about this simple knowledge. We are changing bodies every moment—that is a medical fact. After leaving this body, we will have to accept another body. How are we going to accept that body? What kind of body? This can also be known. For example, if someone is being educated, one can understand that when he passes his examination he is going to be an engineer or medical practitioner. Similarly, in this life, you can prepare yourself to become something in the next life.

Barbara [*Bob's wife*]**:** Can we decide what we want to be in the next life?

Śrīla Prabhupāda: Yes, you can decide. We have decided that in the next life we are going to Kṛṣṇa. This is our decision—to go back home, back to Godhead. Suppose you decide that you are going to be an engineer or a medical practitioner. With that objective you prepare and educate yourself. Similarly, you can decide what you are going to do in the next life. But if you don't decide, then the material nature will decide.

Barbara: Could I have been Kṛṣṇa conscious in my last life? Is it possible that in my last life I was a Kṛṣṇa devotee and have come back again?

Śrīla Prabhupāda: It doesn't matter. But you can become a Kṛṣṇa devotee now. Take advantage of our Kṛṣṇa consciousness movement. When one is perfectly Kṛṣṇa conscious, he does not come back. But if there is a little deficiency, then there is a possibility of coming back. But even though there is a deficiency, he comes back to a nice family. *Śucīnāṁ śrīmatāṁ gehe yoga-bhraṣṭo 'bhijāyate.* ['The unsuccessful *yogī* takes birth in a religious or aristocratic family.'] So human intelligence can decide for the future. An animal cannot. We have discriminatory power: 'If I do this, I will be benefited; if I do that, I will not be benefited.' This power is there in human life. So you have to use it properly. You should know what is the goal of life and decide in that way. That is human civilization.

Barbara: Have you ever seen Kṛṣṇa?

Śrīla Prabhupāda: Yes.

Barbara: You have?

Śrīla Prabhupāda: Daily. At every moment.

Barbara: But not in the material body?

Śrīla Prabhupāda: He has no material body.

Barbara: Well, in the temple here they have pictures of Kṛṣṇa.

Śrīla Prabhupāda: That is not a material body. You are seeing materially because you have material eyes. Because you have material eyes, you cannot see the spiritual form. Therefore Kṛṣṇa kindly appears to be in a material body so that you can see Him. But because He has kindly made Himself just fit for your seeing, that does not mean He has a material body. Suppose the President of the United States kindly comes to your house. That does not mean his position and your position are the same. It is his kindness. Out of love, he may come to your house, but that does not mean he is on the same level as you. Similarly, because we cannot see Kṛṣṇa with our present eyes, He therefore appears before us as a painting, or as a form made of stone or wood. And Kṛṣṇa is not different from these paintings and wood because everything is Kṛṣṇa.

Barbara: After we die, what happens to our spirit?

Śrīla Prabhupāda: You get another body.

Barbara: Immediately?

Śrīla Prabhupāda: Yes. It is just like when you change your apartment: you fix up your new apartment first; then you leave this one and go there.

Barbara: So do we know what type of body we will get?

Śrīla Prabhupāda: Yes, provided you are qualified. Those who are qualified know. But for those who do not know, nature will arrange things. If you do not know, this means you have not prepared your life. So at the time of death your mentality will create another body, and nature will supply it.

Bob: If Kṛṣṇa controls everything, how does Kṛṣṇa control a nondevotee?

Śrīla Prabhupāda: By *māyā.* Kṛṣṇa controls this world just as the government controls everything. A kingdom is controlled by the king's departments.

Bob: And how does Kṛṣṇa control a devotee?

Śrīla Prabhupāda: Just as you control your beloved. For example, if you have a beloved child, you control him for his benefit. If he is going to touch fire, you will immediately tell him, 'No, no, my dear child. Don't touch it.' So a Kṛṣṇa conscious person, a devotee, is never misled, because Kṛṣṇa is always guiding him, whereas those who are not Kṛṣṇa conscious are in the charge of *māyā,* and *māyā* will do the needful, as you have seen.

Bob: Is the time that we'll die preset when we're born? When I'm born, do I have a certain given life span?

Śrīla Prabhupāda: Yes.
A devotee: And he cannot change that?
Śrīla Prabhupāda: No, he cannot change it, but Kṛṣṇa can change it.
Devotee: If he commits suicide, is that also preset?
Śrīla Prabhupāda: Not preset. That you can do because you have a little independence. It is not natural to commit suicide. But because we have independence, we can go from nature to 'un-nature.' A prisoner cannot go out of the prison house naturally. But if somehow or other he arranges to jump over the wall and escapes, then he becomes eligible for further imprisonment. He will be arrested again, and his term of imprisonment will be increased. So, naturally we cannot violate destiny. But if we do it, then we will suffer. But our destiny can be changed by Kṛṣṇa when we are Kṛṣṇa conscious. We do not do it, but Kṛṣṇa will do it. Kṛṣṇa says, *ahaṁ tvāṁ sarva-pāpebhyo mokṣayiṣyāmi:* 'I shall give you protection.' That change takes place for my protection.

There are two categories—nondevotee and devotee. The nondevotee is under the control of material nature, and the devotee is under the direct control of Kṛṣṇa. There are many employees in a big company, and they are controlled by the head of the company through different departmental superintendents. But although outside of home he controls his employees indirectly, the same man at home is controlling his children directly. But he is always a controller.

Similarly, God is always the controller. When one becomes a devotee, he is controlled by God; when he is a nondevotee, he is controlled by God's agent, *māyā.* But one has to be controlled. For example, every citizen of America is controlled by the government. When a citizen is all right, the civil department controls him; when he is not all right, the criminal department controls him. But he cannot say, 'I am not controlled.' That is not possible. Everyone is controlled. If somebody says 'I am not controlled,' he is crazy. Everyone is controlled. So either you will be controlled directly by God, or you will be controlled by His agent, *māyā.* If you choose to be controlled by *māyā,* you spoil your life: you remain in material existence birth after birth, changing your bodies. But if you choose to be controlled by God, then after this body you go back home, back to Godhead. Then your life is successful. You cannot exist without being controlled; that is not possible.

Intelligence means to choose to be controlled by Kṛṣṇa. That is stated in the *Bhagavad-gītā: bahūnāṁ janmanām ante jñānavān māṁ prapadyate.* 'After many births of speculating, one surrenders unto Me.' *Vāsudevaḥ sarvam iti.* One thinks, 'Kṛṣṇa, You are everything. So I have come before You. Please accept me. I am now fully surrendered unto You, so please control me. For so long I have been controlled by these rascal senses, without any benefit. Under the control of the senses I have served so-called family, society, country, nation—up to serving the dogs. But nothing has given me satisfaction. But now I have had the good sense to put myself under Your control. Instead of being controlled by dog, let me be controlled by God.' This is Kṛṣṇa consciousness. Have you not seen how a man is controlled by a dog? In the street the dog stops to pass stool, and his master will stand and wait. Is it not? The dog is passing stool and urine, and the man is thinking, 'I am the master.' But he is being controlled by the dog! That is *māyā.* What do you think? Has he not become controlled by the dog?

Bob: That is so.

Śrīla Prabhupāda: But he is thinking, 'I am the master of the dog.' A family man is controlled by his wife, his children, his servants, everyone, but he is thinking, 'I am master.' President Nixon is thinking that he is master of his country, but he is controlled. At once he can be dismissed by the public, his servants! At election time he will take a position, claiming, 'I will give you very good service,' and 'I shall be a first-class servant.' Therefore people vote, 'All right, you become president.' And he is advertising: 'Reelect me! Reelect me!' That means he is a servant. But he is thinking, 'I am the master.' That is illusion, *māyā.* One who is controlled by *māyā* thinks himself the master while he is a servant. But a devotee never thinks, 'I am the master,' only 'I am Kṛṣṇa's servant.' That is *mukti,* liberation. A devotee is never controlled by false thoughts. He knows his position—*svarūpena vyavasthitiḥ. Mukti,* liberation, means to be situated in one's own constitutional position as a servant of Kṛṣṇa. So if I know that I am a servant of Kṛṣṇa, that is my liberation. And if I think that I am the master, that is bondage. This is the difference between liberated life and conditioned life.

So these Kṛṣṇa conscious devotees are always thinking that they are servants of Kṛṣṇa. Therefore they are all liberated. They do not endeavour for liberation. They are already liberated because they are situated in their constitutional position.

Bob: Prabhupāda, some religious people claim that Jesus is guiding them. Can this be so?

Śrīla Prabhupāda: Yes, but they are not taking the guidance. Jesus is guiding the Christians, telling them, 'Thou shalt not kill,' but they are killing. So how are they following Jesus' guidance? Simply saying 'I am guided by Jesus Christ, but I don't care for his words'—will that do? Is that guidance? Nobody is being guided by Jesus Christ. Their claim is false. It is very hard to find a man who is actually being guided by Jesus Christ. Jesus Christ's guidance is available, but nobody is caring for him. They have taken Jesus Christ as contractor to take up their sins. That is their philosophy. They commit all kinds of sins, and poor Jesus Christ will be responsible. That is their religion. Therefore they say, 'We have a very good religion. For all our sinful activities, Jesus Christ will die.' Is that good religion? They have no sympathy for Jesus Christ. If they did they would think, 'He died for our sins. Why should we commit sins again? Such a great life has been sacrificed for our sins, so we should be guided by Jesus Christ.' But they take it otherwise: 'Ah, I shall go on committing all sins, and Jesus Christ has made a contract to nullify all my sins; I'll simply go to the church and confess and come back and again do all nonsense.' Do you think that shows very good intelligence?

Bob: No.
Śrīla Prabhupāda: One who is actually guided by Jesus Christ will certainly get liberation. But it is very hard to find a man who is actually being guided by Jesus Christ.
Bob: What about the 'Jesus freaks,' young people who read the Bible very often?
Śrīla Prabhupāda: But violence is against the Bible's injunctions. How can they kill if they are following the Bible?
Bob: They claim that the Bible says Jesus ate meat.
Śrīla Prabhupāda: That's all right. He may eat anything; he is powerful. But he has ordered, 'Thou shalt not kill. You must stop killing.' He is powerful. He can eat the whole world. But you cannot compare yourself to Jesus Christ. You cannot imitate him; you have to abide by his order. Then you are guided by Jesus Christ. That is actual obedience. The *Bhāgavatam* explains that one who is an *īśvara,* who is empowered, can do anything, but that we cannot imitate. We have to abide by his order.

Admitting that Jesus ate meat, you do not know under what conditions he ate meat. He advised others not to kill, yet he himself ate meat. Do you think Jesus Christ was contradicting himself?
Bob: No.
Śrīla Prabhupāda: He cannot do that. That is real faith in him—to understand that he cannot do that. So why did he eat meat? He has his reasons why, but he has asked me not to kill. Therefore I have to follow. That is the real system. You are not Jesus Christ; you cannot imitate him. He has sacrificed his life for God. Can you do that? Why imitate Jesus Christ only by eating meat? Why not imitate Jesus Christ by sacrificing your life for spreading God consciousness? They are so-called Christians, but what are they doing for God? Consider how the sun is absorbing urine. Can you drink urine? If you want to imitate the sun and drink urine, can you? Similarly, Jesus Christ is so powerful he can do anything. But we cannot imitate; we have to simply abide by his order. That is real Christianity. It is wrong to imitate a powerful man.

Our Vedic literature describes that once there was an ocean of poison and no one knew what to do with it. Then Lord Śiva said, 'All right, I'll drink it.' So he drank the whole poison ocean and kept it in his throat. Now, can you drink poison? Not the whole ocean, just one cup. Lord Śiva never advised that we drink poison. So you have to abide by his advice, not try to imitate him. These LSD and marijuana people say that Lord Śiva used to smoke *gañjā* [hashish]. But Lord Śiva drank a whole ocean of poison! Can you do that?

It is Lord Śiva's *instructions* that should be followed, not his example of smoking *gañjā*. When Pārvatī asked him what method of worship is best, he said, *viṣṇor ārādhanaṁ param:* 'The best worship is worship of Lord Viṣṇu, Kṛṣṇa.' There are many demigods, but he recommended Viṣṇu worship as the best. And better than Viṣṇu worship, he said, is worship of a Vaiṣṇava. The exact word he used is *tadīyānām*—'those who are related to Viṣṇu.' For instance, we worship the Tulasī plant. We do not worship all plants, but because Tulasī has a very intimate connection with Kṛṣṇa, or Viṣṇu, we worship her. Similarly, if anything is intimately related with Kṛṣṇa, worship of that thing is better than worship of Viṣṇu.

Bob: Why is that?

Śrīla Prabhupāda: Because Kṛṣṇa will be pleased. Suppose you have a dog and some friend comes and pats your dog and says, 'My, what a nice dog you have.' [*Śrīla Prabhupāda makes big patting motions amidst general laughter.*] You become pleased and think, 'Oh, he is my good friend.' You see? [*Some Indian guests enter the room.*]

Please have some *prasādam.*

[*Śrīla Prabhupāda continues speaking with his guests, sometimes in English and sometimes in Hindi. It is his last day in New York, and his plane to London is scheduled to leave in only a few hours. Bob has brought a car to drive Śrīla Prabhupāda to Kennedy Airport. The devotees are scurrying about, bringing luggage to the car, putting the manuscripts of Śrīla Prabhupāda's latest translating work in order, and making other last-minute arrangements.*]

Śyāmasundara: Everything's ready, Śrīla Prabhupāda. The car is waiting for us.

Śrīla Prabhupāda: So? We can go now? All right. Hare Kṛṣṇa!

Concluding Words

Between 1972 and 1976 I took to heart Śrīla Prabhupāda's suggestion that I make a serious study of the *Bhagavad-gītā* and *bhakti-yoga*. He advised me to continue asking questions from different angles of vision, and to consult with others on the *bhakti* path. Though I was anxious to acquire the devotional taste I saw in his disciples, I was determined to approach my study of *bhakti-yoga* cautiously and deliberately.

As a scientist, I first explored the *Gītā's* epistemology. The "science" of *bhakti-yoga* has its own tools and methods for understanding transcendental subjects. I felt the need to overcome my skepticism enough to experiment with these tools, which include meditative chanting and hearing about Kṛṣṇa. Śrīla Prabhupāda had convinced me enough to take that necessary first step; my own unexpectedly sweet experiences convinced me to continue further.

On July 19, 1976, some four years after our meeting, Śrīla Prabhupāda accepted my wife and I as his disciples. In keeping with the ancient *Vaiṣṇava* tradition, he initiated us as Bhakti Devī Dāsī and Brahmatīrtha Dāsa—names indicating that we had become *sādhakas*, serious aspirants on the spiritual path.

Since 1972, when my adventure with Krishna began, I have always tried to balance my inner life with my external responsibilities. The loving support of my wife and the mentorship of many expert practitioners have helped ground me in the principles of the *Gītā*.

One of these principles is to connect (the word *yoga* literally means "to connect") with our inner voice, the higher voice known in Sanskrit as *Paramātmā* and in pop culture as "the Force." Building this intuitive connection has brought me strength in all facets of my life. How is such an intuitive connection built? With philosophical understanding, chanting, and applying the *Gītā's* systems of checking intuition with trusted external sources.

While developing my career as a scientist and consultant, I participated directly in *bhakti-yoga* practices through the International Society for Krishna Consciousness, the society founded by Śrīla Prabhupāda. My services in the Society have included heading up a children's school, publishing books, and encouraging the academic study of the principles of *bhakti-yoga*. These opportunities have deepened and enriched my perception of *bhakti-yoga*, and that perception has continued to grow since Śrīla Prabhupāda so perfectly answered my fumbling questions thirty-three years ago.

Brahmatīrtha Dāsa (Bob Cohen)
Gainesville, Florida
June 24, 2005

His Divine Grace
A.C. Bhaktivedanta Swami
Prabhupāda

His Divine Grace A.C. Bhaktivedanta Swami Prabhupāda appeared in this world in 1896 in Calcutta, India. He first met his spiritual master, Śrīla Bhaktisiddhānta Sarasvatī Gosvāmī, in Calcutta in 1922. Bhaktisiddhānta Sarasvatī was a prominent religious scholar and the founder of the Gauḍīya Maṭha (a *Vaiṣṇava* movement with sixty-four centers) in India. He liked this educated young man and convinced him to dedicate his life to teaching Vedic knowledge. Śrīla Prabhupāda became his student and, in 1933, received initiation as his disciple.

At their first meeting Śrīla Bhaktisiddhānta Sarasvatī requested Śrīla Prabhupāda to broadcast Vedic knowledge in English. In the years that followed, Śrīla Prabhupāda wrote a commentary on the *Bhagavad-gītā* and assisted the Gauḍīya Maṭha in its work. In 1944, he started *Back to Godhead,* a fortnightly magazine in English. Singlehandedly, Śrīla Prabhupāda edited it, typed the manuscripts, checked the galley proofs, and even distributed the individual copies. The magazine now continues to be published by his disciples throughout the world in different languages.

In 1950, Śrīla Prabhupāda retired from domestic life to devote more time to his studies and writing. He traveled to the holy town of Vṛndāvana, where he lived in humble circumstances in the historic temple of Rādhā-Dāmodara. There, for several years, he engaged in deep study and writing. He accepted the renounced order of life (*sannyāsa*) in 1959. It was at the Rādhā-Dāmodara temple that Śrīla Prabhupāda began to work on his life's masterpiece: a multivolume translation of the eighteen-thousand-verse *Śrīmad-Bhāgavatam* (*Bhāgavata Purāṇa*) with full commentary. After publishing three volumes of the *Bhāgavatam,* Śrīla Prabhupāda traveled by freighter to New York City. He was practically penniless, but had faith that the mission of his spiritual master could be successful. On the day he landed in America and saw the gray mists hanging over the towering skyscrapers, he penned these words in his diary: "My dear Lord Kṛṣṇa, I am sure that when this transcendental message penetrates their hearts, they will certainly feel gladdened and thus become liberated from all unhappy conditions of life." He was sixty-nine years old, alone and with few resources, but the wealth of spiritual knowledge and devotion he possessed was an unwavering source of strength and inspiration.

"At a very advanced age, when most people would be resting on their laurels," writes Harvey Cox, Harvard University theologian and author, "Śrīla Prabhupāda harkened to the mandate of his own spiritual teacher and set out on the difficult and demanding voyage to America. Śrīla Prabhupāda is, of course, only one of thousands of teachers. But in another sense, he is one in a thousand, maybe one in a million."

In 1966, Śrīla Prabhupāda founded the International Society for Krishna Consciousness, which became the formal name for the Hare Kṛṣṇa movement.

In the years that followed, Śrīla Prabhupāda gradually attracted tens of thousands of followers, started more than a hundred temples and *āśramas,* and published scores of books. His achievement is remarkable in that he transplanted India's ancient spiritual culture to the twentieth-century Western world.

In 1968, Śrīla Prabhupāda sent three devotee couples to bring Kṛṣṇa consciousness to the U.K. At first, these devotees were cared for by Hindu families who appreciated their mission, but soon they became well known in London for the street-chanting on Oxford Street. A headline in the *Times* announced, "Kṛṣṇa Chant Startles London." But the *mahā-mantra* soon became popular. Former Beatle George Harrison, who had known Śrīla Prabhupāda and the chanting before the devotees came to England, wanted to help. He arranged to produce a recording of the *mantra* on the Beatles' Apple label. It reached the Top Ten in Britain and number one in some other countries.

When Śrīla Prabhupāda arrived in England, he was the guest of John Lennon at his estate in Tittenhurst, while work was progressing on the temple in Bloomsbury, near the British Museum. In November 1969, Śrīla Prabhupāda opened the temple—the first Rādhā-Kṛṣṇa temple in Europe. The movement grew from strength to strength. Once again, George Harrison offered to help by donating a beautiful mock-Tudor manor house and estate in Hertfordshire. Now named Bhaktivedanta Manor, it is the Society's main training center in Britain.

New devotees of Kṛṣṇa soon became highly visible in all the major cities around the world by their public chanting and their distribution of Śrīla Prabhupāda's books of Vedic knowledge. They began staging joyous cultural festivals throughout the year and serving millions of plates of delicious food offered to Kṛṣṇa (known as *prasādam*) throughout the world. As a result, ISKCON has significantly influenced the lives of hundreds of thousands of people. The late A.L. Basham, one of the world's leading authorities on Indian history and culture, wrote, "The Hare Kṛṣṇa movement arose out of next to nothing in less than twenty years and has become known all over the West. This is an important fact in the history of the Western world."

In just twelve years, despite his advanced age, Śrīla Prabhupāda circled the globe fourteen times on lecture tours that took him to six continents. Yet this vigorous schedule did not slow his prolific literary output. His writings constitute a veritable library of Vedic philosophy, religion, literature, and culture.

Indeed, Śrīla Prabhupāda's most significant contribution is his books. Highly respected by academics for their authority, depth, and clarity, they are used as textbooks in numerous university courses.

Garry Gelade, a professor at Oxford University's Department of Philosophy, wrote of them: "These texts are to be treasured. No one of whatever faith or philosophical persuasion who reads these books with an open mind can fail to be moved and impressed." And Dr. Larry Shinn, Dean of the College of Arts and Sciences at Bucknell University, wrote, "Prabhupāda's personal piety gave him real authority. He exhibited complete command of the scriptures, an unusual depth of realization, and an outstanding personal example, because he actually lived what he taught."

Śrīla Prabhupāda's writings have been translated into over 80 languages. The Bhaktivedanta Book Trust, established in 1972 to publish his works, has thus become the world's largest publisher of books in the field of Indian religion and philosophy. 480 million copies have been sold to date.

Before he passed away on the 14th of November 1977, Srila Prabhupāda had guided that Society and seen it grow to a worldwide confederation of more than one hundred *āśramas,* schools, temples, institutes, and farm communities.

Centres of the International Society for Krishna Consciousness

Founder-*Ācārya:* His Divine Grace A. C. Bhaktivedanta Swami Prabhupāda

For further information on classes, programmes, festivals, residential courses and local meetings, please contact the centre nearest you.

UNITED KINGDOM & IRELAND

Belfast — Sri Sri Radha-Madhava Mandir, Brooklands, 140 Upper Dunmurray Lane, Belfast, BT17 0HE / Tel: +44 (0)28 9062 0530 / e-mail: belfast@iskcon.org.uk

Birmingham — 84 Stanmore Rd, Edgbaston, Birmingham, B16 9TB / Tel: +44 (0)121 420 4999 e-mail: birmingham@iskcon.org.uk / web: iskconbirmingham.org

Cardiff — The Soul Centre, 116, Cowbridge Road, Cardiff, CF11 00X / Tel: +44 (0)20 0301 e-mail: the.soul.centre@pamho.net / web: www.iskconwales.org

Coventry — Kingfield Rd, Coventry (mail: 19 Gloucester St, Coventry CV1 3BZ) Tel: +44 (0)24 7655 2822 or 5420 / e-mail: haridas.kds@pamho.net

Dublin — For info telephone +353 (0) 87 992 1332 / e-mail: praghosa.sdg@pamho.net

Glasgow — Karuna Bhavan, Bankhouse Rd, Lesmahagow, Lanarkshire, ML11 0ES Tel: +44 (0) 1555 894526 / e-mail: karunabhavan@aol.com

Leicester — 21 Thoresby St, North Evington, Leicester, LE5 4GU / Tel & fax: +44 (0)116 276 2587 / e-mail: pradyumna.jas@pamho.net / web: www.iskconleicester.com

London (central) — Sri Sri Radha-Krishna Temple, 10 Soho St, London, W1D 3DL Tel: +44 (0)20 7437 3662 / Fax: +44 (0)20 7439 1127 / e-mail: london@pamho.net web: www.iskcon-london.com

London (south) — 42 Enmore Rd, South Norwood, London, SE25 5NG Tel: +44 (0)20 8656 4296

Manchester — 20 Mayfield Rd, Whalley Range, Manchester, M16 8FT Tel: +44 (0)161 226 4416

Newcastle-upon-Tyne — 304 Westgate Rd, Newcastle-upon-Tyne, NE4 6AR Tel: +44 (0)191 272 1911 / e-mail: bhakti.rasa@pamho.net

Scotland — Karuna Bhavan, Bankhouse Rd, Lesmahagow, Lanarkshire, ML11 0ES Tel: +44 (0)1555 894790 / Fax: +44 (0)1555 894526 / e-mail: karuna.bhavan@aol.com web: www.gouranga.cc

Swansea — The Hare Krishna Temple, 8 Craddock St, Swansea, SA1 3EN / Tel: +44 (0)1792 468469 / e-mail: iskcon.swansea@pamho.net / web: www.iskconwales.org

Watford — Bhaktivedanta Manor, Hilfield Lane, Watford, WD25 8EZ / Tel: +44 (0)1923 857244 Fax: +44 (0)1923 852896 / e-mail: bhaktivedanta.manor@pamho.net web: www.krishnatemple.com

RURAL COMMUNITIES

Upper Lough Erne (Northern Ireland) — Govindadwipa Dharma, Inisrath Island, Derrylin, Co. Fermanagh, BT92 9GN / Tel: +44 (0)28 6772 1512 / e-mail: govindadwipa@pamho.net

RESTAURANTS

Dublin — Govinda's, 4 Aungier St, Dublin 2, Irish Republic Tel: +353 (0)1 475 0309 e-mail: praghosa.sdg@pamho.net / web: www.govindas.ie

Dublin — Govinda's, 83 Middle Abbey St, Dublin 1, Irish Republic / Tel: +358 (0)1 8729861 e-mail: praghosa.sdg@pamho.net

London — Govinda's, 10 Soho St, London, W1D 3DL / Tel: +44 (0)20 7437 4928 e-mail: govindas@iskconlondon.org

Swansea — Govinda's, 8 Craddock St, Swansea, SA1 3EN Tel: +44 (0)1792 468469 e-mail: govin_das@hotmail.com

Hare Krishna meetings are held regularly in more than 40 towns in the UK. For more information, contact: ISKCON Reader Services, P.O. Box 730, Watford, WD25 8ZE Website: www.iskcon.org.uk

OTHER COUNTRIES

Abentheuer, Germany — Böckingstr. 8, 55767 Abentheuer / Tel: +49 (0)6782 980436
Fax: 980437 / e-mail: goloka.dhama.temple@pamho.net

Amsterdam, The Netherlands — Van Hilligaertstraat 17hs, 1072 JX Amsterdam
Tel: +31 (0)20 675-1404 / Fax: +31 (0)20 675-1405 / e-mail: www.iskcon.nl
www.harekrsna.nl

Budapest, Hungary — Hare Krishna Temple, 1039 Budapest (Csillaghegy), Lehel utca 15-17.
Tel/fax: +36 1 391 0435 / e-mail: budapest@pamho.net

Budapest, Hungary — Govinda's Restaurant, 1051 Budapest, Vigyázó Ferenc u. 4.
Tel: +36 1 473 1309, +36 1 269 1625

Durban, South Africa — 50 Bhaktivedanta Swami Circle (mail: P.O. Box 56003)
Chatsworth, 4030 Durban / Tel: +27 (0)31 403-3328 / Fax: +27 (0)31 403-4429
e-mail: iskcon.kzn@pamho.net

Durbuy, Belgium — Château de Petite Somme, 6940 Durbuy (Septon)
Tel: +32 (0)86 322926 / Fax: +32 (0)86 322929 / e-mail: radhadesh@pamho.net
www.radhadesh.com

Florence, Italy (Villa Vrindavan) — Via Comunale Scopeti 108, 50026 San Casciano
in Val di Pesa (Fl) / Tel: +39 055 820054 / Fax: +39 055 828470

Grödinge, Sweden (New Radhakunda) — Korsnäs Gård, 14792 Grödinge
Tel: +46 (0)8 530-29800 / Fax: +46 (0)8 530-25062 / e-mail: info@pamho.net

Guadalajara, Spain (New Vraja Mandala) — (Santa Clara) Brihuega, Guadalajara
Tel: +34 949 280436 / e-mail: vraj.eco.vill@pamho.net / www.madhuvan.org

Los Angeles, USA — 3764 Watseka Ave., Los Angeles CA 90034 / Tel: +1 310 836-2676
Fax: +1 310 839-2715 / e-mail: svavasa.acbsp@pamho.net

Mayapur, India — Sri Mayapur Chandrodaya Mandir, P.O. Shree Mayapur Dham,
Nadia District, W.B. 741 313 / Tel: +91 (0)3472-245239 / Fax: (0)3472-245238
e-mail: mayapur.chandrodaya@pamho.net / www.mayapur.info, www.mayapurnews.com

Mumbai, India (Bombay) — Hare Krishna Land, Juhu 400 049 / Tel: +91 (22) 2620-6860
Fax: +91 (22) 2620-5214 / e-mail: iskcon.juhu@pamho.net / www.iskconmumbai.com

New Delhi, India — Sant Nagar Main Rd. (Garhi), behind Nehru Place Complex
(mail: P. O. Box 7061), 110 065 New Delhi / Tel: (011) 623-5133 / Fax: (011) 6221-5421
or 628-0067 / e-mail: kratu.acbsp@pamho.net

New York, USA — 305 Schermerhorn St., Brooklyn, New York 11217 / Tel: +1 718 855-6714
Fax: +1 718 875-6127 / e-mail: ramabhadra@aol.com

Paris, France — 33 rue du docteur Jean Vaquier, 93160 Noisy le Grand
Tel. / fax: +33 (0)1 4303-0951 / e-mail: param.gati.swami@pamho.net

Somogyvámos, Hungary — Krishna Valley, Indian Cultural Centre and Biofarm,
8669 Somogyvámos, Fó u. 38. / Tel: +36 85 540 002, +36 30 377 1530
e-mail: info@krisna-volgy.hu

Stockholm, Sweden — Fridhemsgatan 22, 11240 Stockholm / Tel: +46 (0)8 654-9002
Fax: +46 (0)8 650-8813 / e-mail: tapasa.rns@pamho.net

Sydney, Australia — 180 Falcon St., North Sydney, NSW 2060 (mail: P.O. Box 459,
Cammeray, NSW 2062) / Tel: +61 (2) 9959-4558 / Fax: +61 (2) 9957-1893
e-mail: info@iskcon.com.au / www.iskcon.com.au

Vrindavan, India — Krishna-Balaram Mandir, Bhaktivedanta Swami Marg, Raman Reti,
Vrindavan, Mathura District, U.P. 281 124 / Tel: +91 (0)565 442596 / Fax: +91 (0)565
442574 / e-mail: mahaman@pamho.net

Zürich, Switzerland — Bergstrasse 54, 8030 Zürich / Tel: +41 (0) 44 262 33 88
Fax: +41 (0) 44 262 31 14 / e-mail: kgs@pamho.net / www.krishna.ch

This is a partial list of centres. For a full list, please contact one of the above addresses or visit us on the web at www.iskcon.com or www.krishna.com.